Comm
Messag
and Prof

AVOIDING PLAGIARISM

Valerie A. Gray

Harrisburg Area Community College

Kendall Hunt
publishing company

Kendall Hunt
publishing company

www.kendallhunt.com
Send all inquiries to:
4050 Westmark Drive
Dubuque, IA 52004-1840

ISBN 978-1-4652-0301-4

Printed in the United States of America
10   9   8   7   6   5   4   3   2   1

Contents

Introduction

Content

Let us start with the basics. This textbook is composed to help you discover how to write with academic and professional integrity. The book engages students by asking and requiring them to think critically about the sources they use, consider the reliability and implications for using information, think about how they would justify their choices, and apply language and standards for academic writing. It also contains elements of heuristics (aids to learning and problem-solving) to help students discover and apply concepts.

The book is an interactive text. As students are prompted to think about issues regarding academic honesty, they can comment directly in the text. This book uses a call-and-respond approach; when a question is asked or a task presented, students are required to respond in "real time." Therefore, instructors are encouraged to engage students as they discuss and present various topics in the textbook.

Organization

The book first asks students to explore their perceptions of academic dishonesty. A survey prompts them to think about how they feel and react to academic dishonesty situations. Next, students learn about the origins of plagiarism and famous cases of plagiarism in academics and professions. Chapter One provides ten tips students can implement to help them avoid plagiarism. From the first chapter, students learn the importance of citing, documenting, incorporating, and verifying in research writing. Chapter Two provides an introduction to conducting research and synthesizing data. Chapter Three contains the citation and documentation style for some of the most commonly used sources. Chapter Four presents ethical standards for collaborative writing and business writing. Chapter Five provides insight on how social media, the arts, and popular culture all influence our perception of academic and professional honesty.

Text Boxes

Application text boxes appear throughout the book. They serve the purpose of immediate application; after a topic is presented, an application box or an ethical reflection box appears in which students must respond. Responding in the book serves as a way for students to journal their reactions—whether ethical or unethical—so that they will reflect on past decisions to help them in the future.

Terminology

The book uses the active voice to speak directly to the reader. *You* refers to the reader of the text. *Originator* refers to the writer of the source text. *Writer* refers to the person who must write the majority of the text and who incorporates originators' sources to support the writer's text.

Glossary

Various terms appear in the text; however, readers may be unfamiliar with the definitions for each term, which are not included within the text. The glossary contains these definitions.

Part One

Writing with Integrity

It is essential for you to find your own compositional voice and develop effective research strategies as you incorporate sources. Consequently, when you commit academic and professional dishonesty by, for example, plagiarizing, cheating, or committing copyright infringement, you are doing a disservice to yourself, the university, and the company you represent. Part One focuses on writing with integrity and incorporating sources.

Chapter One describes the history of citing and documenting, ethical codes of conduct, format for MLA and APA citations, and academic and professional honesty standards. Also presented are the cases of high-profile individuals who have committed plagiarism and why they did so. This information is presented as discussion points to further help you avoid plagiarism. Chapter Two presents information about how to test the reliability of sources, how to synthesize sources, and how to use techniques and tips for incorporating sources. Chapter Three focuses on when to use a quote, paraphrase, or summary.

Numerous professional articles are included as reading and researching prompts to promote critical thinking. When you read an article, it often will lead you to think about other topics to investigate further. These activities will help you practice expanding an idea, taking the opposite position from the author, or formulating a totally different research area that better fits your needs.

Part One, therefore, serves as a historical, practical, and applicable orientation to academic and professional honesty. Questions, textboxes, and activities appear throughout the chapters to help you develop strategies for applying academic and professional honesty standards to your writing. Additional assignments appear at the end of each chapter.

CHAPTER 1

Follow Academic Honesty Standards

The writing process involves several steps. In its basic form, it entails prewriting (brainstorming, planning, outlining, and researching), drafting (writing), and revising (editing, reorganizing, and proofreading). Each step is equally important. Once you have completed the written work, typed your name, and submitted the assignment to your professor, you have claimed ownership. Therefore, you want to ensure that you have represented the information appropriately.

Chapter Objectives

After reading this chapter and completing the exercises, you will be able to:

- Define academic honesty and its associated terms.
- Differentiate between citation and documentation.
- Understand the standards of academic honesty.
- Understand how to apply the standards of academic honesty.

You will compose a variety of documents throughout your academic and professional careers that require sources. These documents can run the gamut of, for example:

- Research reports
- Recommendation reports
- Memos
- Letters
- Literature reviews
- Critiques
- Critical analyses
- Comparisons
- Presentations
- Annotated bibliographies
- Class discussions
- News stories

These fact-based documents will require you to conduct research and incorporate sources to support your position, solve a problem, and present information. Regardless of the document, if you use sources, you must use them appropriately and you must cite and document each.

Rate Your Academic Honesty IQ—Pretest

What is academic honesty? What is plagiarism? Why do students commit academic offenses? How can you prevent plagiarism? What are the signs of plagiarism? Test your knowledge. Knowing your perception of academic honesty will help you understand how to write with academic honesty.

Take a few moments to answer these questions. Honestly present your beliefs. After you answer the questions, complete the following survey.

The purpose of this survey is to measure your knowledge of academic dishonesty and to determine reasons why students commit plagiarism (the offering of someone else's work, words, or idea as your own or using material from another source without acknowledgement—that is, without giving credit to the originator).

Note: You will find detailed information for each question topic in Chapter One. You will also find another copy of this IQ at the end of the chapter to test how your knowledge has increased.

What is plagiarism?

When were you first introduced to the term plagiarism?

What did you learn about plagiarism?

Check the statements regarding plagiarism that you think are true.

_____ If 50% or more of a paper is from sources and I correctly cite and document the sources, I have not committed plagiarism.

_____ If 25% or more of a paper is from sources and I correctly cite and document the sources, I have not committed plagiarism.

_____ I can write a paper for one class and submit the same paper (or with minor modification) for another class.

_____	Students commit plagiarism because they do not know what it is.
_____	Students commit plagiarism because they do not think they will get caught.
_____	Students commit plagiarism because they do not care about the ramifications.
_____	Students commit plagiarism because they do not have time to write the paper.
_____	Students who give or receive answers for any assignment or use devices or documents prohibited by the instructor are committing plagiarism.
_____	Students who falsify documents to take an examine for someone else are committing plagiarism.
_____	Students who use and/or submit the work of another as their own are committing plagiarism.
_____	Students who buy or sell essays, research papers, assignments, laboratory assignments, computer programs, or any class-related information are committing plagiarism.
_____	Students falsifying their own or another's academic records, or falsifying of admissions, registration, or other related college materials are committing plagiarism.

Students in English 106 Written Business Communication completed this survey in spring 2011. Compare your responses. The percentage refers to the percentage of students who agreed with the statement. What conclusion can you surmise from this data?

Check the statements regarding plagiarism that you think are true.	
49%	If 50% or more of a paper is from sources and I correctly cite and document the sources, I have not committed plagiarism.
40%	If 25% or more of a paper is from sources and I correctly cite and document the sources, I have not committed plagiarism.
35%	I can write a paper for one class and submit the same paper (or with minor modification) for another class.

51%	Students commit plagiarism because they do not know what it is.
98%	Students commit plagiarism because they do not think they will get caught.
80%	Students commit plagiarism because they do not care about the ramifications.
60%	Students commit plagiarism because they do not have time to write the paper.
65%	Students who give or receive answers for any assignment or use devices or documents prohibited by the instructor are committing plagiarism.
62%	Students who falsify documents to take an examine for someone else are committing plagiarism.
51%	Students who use and/or submit the work of another as their own are committing plagiarism.
82%	Students who buy or sell essays, research papers, assignments, laboratory assignments, computer programs, or any class-related information are committing plagiarism.
62%	Students falsifying their own or another's academic records, or falsifying of admissions, registration, or other related college materials are committing plagiarism.

What is Academic Dishonesty?

Academic dishonesty is an intentional act of deception in which writers (students, professors, professionals, and lay writers) claim credit for the work or effort of another person, use unauthorized material, or fabricate information in any academic or professional work.

Students often commit academic dishonesty unintentionally. Examples of unintentional academic dishonesty include forgetting to use quotation marks or neglecting to acknowledge a source in the body of an essay or on the bibliographic page. Although these acts may be unintentional, they do not automatically absolve students from being accused of academic dishonesty. Regardless of intent, if information is not cited properly, the student has, nonetheless, misrepresented the information. Misrepresentation means not applying what you know or what you should have known to a particular situation. Why would unintentional academic dishonesty be considered misrepresentation? Academic dishonesty is widely discussed in secondary and post-secondary education systems. Chances are you were introduced to academic dishonesty at a young age. Academic dishonesty standards are published in student handbooks in colleges and universities throughout the country. Therefore, unintentional plagiarism is not a defense. Plagiarism is the term most associated with academic dishonesty.

What is Plagiarism?

Plagiarism (derived from the English *plagiary*) was first applied to the act of literary theft in 1601. The term originated from the Latin *plagiārius* ("plagiarism"). Literally, plagiarism means literary theft, to steal words.

One of the first accusations of plagiarism was documented in first century A.D. Roman poet Marcus Valerius Martial (c. AD40 – c. 102), composed a book of epigrams (Oxford Reference Online). Epigrams are amusing and clever prose on topics, and his ranged from commentaries of Roman society to the humorous and sublime. It is Epigram Number 52 in which he accuses another poet of claiming his words.

> "To your charge I entrust, Quintianus, my works—if, after all, I can call those mine which that poet of yours recites. If they complain of their grievous servitude, come forward as their champion and give bail for them; and when that fellow calls himself their owner, say that they are mine, sent forth from my hand. If thrice and four times you shout this, you will shame the plagiarist" ("Plagiarism" Issues & Controversies).

High-Profile Cases of Plagiarism

In 2006, then Harvard sophomore Kaavya Viswanathan was a promising new author. Based on projections of her first novel, *Opal Mehta Got Kissed, Got Wild, and Got a Life*, published by Little Brown and Company, she was offered a multi-book contract and movie options. Shortly after the release of her book, she was accused of paraphrasing passages from author Megan McCafferty's first novel *Sloppy Firsts*. Ms.Viswanathan stated that any similarities between the two novels were coincidental. Officials at Little Brown canceled the book deal and removed all copies of the novel from the shelves of book sellers ("Publisher Pulls Harvard Student's Novel Over Alleged Plagiarism").

In March 2008, aide to President George W. Bush and columnist writer Tim Geoglein admitted that he plagiarized several stories (Stolberg).

When Karl-Theodor zu Guttenberg was a doctoral student in 2007, he neglected to cite two passages of his dissertation. In March 2011, while a popular German minister, his act of plagiarism became public. As a result, he lost his position and his ranking as a PhD (Dempsey).

The invention of the moveable type printing press by Johannes Gutenberg in 1440 made it possible to make ideas permanent and led to the dissemination of information to the masses. It also made charges of plagiarism evidential.

Writers analyzed their audiences to determine how to best fit a niche market by developing their writing to showcase how it would benefit the reader. For example, poets wrote in such a way that they would get published so that their works could be read. The mass production of texts expressing various points of view produced contradictions and more information for public discourse. Before 1500, it was normal for text not to have the author's name attached to it (Leitch). The Scientific Revolution marked the Enlightenment period, which was sparked by intellectual insights and the Age of Reason. The new scientific disciplines during Enlightenment marked the period of transition between the old and the new. As scholar Elizabeth Eisenstein described this connection, "Once old texts came together within the same study, diverse systems of ideas and special disciplines could be combined. Increased output directed at relatively stable markets, in short, created conditions that favored new combinations of old ideas at first and then, later on, the creation of entirely new systems of thought" (49).

In the 1600s, the establishment of the Royal Society of London for Improving Natural Knowledge occurred. The society was part of scientific enlightenment; it was the forbearer in the formation of the sciences as academic disciplines and departments. Its members believed in gaining natural knowledge through primary research, specifically, through observations and experimentation ("The Royal Society"). By experiencing knowledge this way, researchers become the authority in the field; thus, they became the content experts.

The cliché "imitation is the best form of flattery" was true through the seventeenth century; writers believed that plagiarism led writers to improve meaning, syntax, and style. Nineteenth-century German poet and literary critic Heinrich Heine expressed that point of view when he declared:

> Nothing is sillier than this charge of plagiarism. There is no sixth commandment in art. The poet dare help himself wherever he lists, wherever he finds material suited to his work. He may even appropriate entire columns with their carved capitals, if the temple he thus supports be a beautiful one ("Plagiarism" Issues & Controversies).

In the eighteenth century, writers began to value their texts as original sources of information. During this time, printing, bookmaking and book selling became a popular and lucrative industry. Thus, writers could receive a monetary return on their writing. Plagiarized work equaled less income. Therefore, accusations of plagiarism were taken seriously. The eighteenth century is also when plagiarism was noticed in universities, as students began to write more and more assignments instead of reciting assignments ("Plagiarism" Issues & Controversies). Then, as now, students felt pressured to compose original essays and conduct new research.

> What are the difficulties college students face that may lead them to commit plagiarism? Identify at least three. You may explain circumstances in which plagiarism takes place.
> 1.
>
> 2.
>
> 3.
>
> 4.
>
> 5.

What Are the Signs of Plagiarism? How Can You Prevent Plagiarism?

Writers commit plagiarism when they use the words originated by other writers without giving those writers credit or attribution. Writers use three primary ways to acknowledge the original source: quoting text, summarizing text, and paraphrasing text.

Quoting Text

Direct quotation refers to taking text from the originator without making any changes. Use a direct quote when the content of the originator's text highlights a point that supports your thesis or argument. A quote is a strong statement of support and emphasizes a point you want the audience to understand. A quote can build credibility when the audience knows and respects the person you are quoting or when a quote makes your point more vivid.

The words and sentences must be encased in quotation marks. However, when the passage is longer than two sentences, the passage is single-spaced and indented at the left and right margins.

Paraphrasing Text

Paraphrasing text refers to putting a passage from the originator into your own words. A passage refers to a segment of written text that is two or three sentences long. Paraphrase the originator's text to clarify a point and expand upon it. When you paraphrase, be sure to change the cadence of the original text. Even though you are paraphrasing, you want your writing style to be present. Why is it necessary to cite a paraphrase? Although you are changing the words, you are restating the originator's main premise, not yours.

Summarizing Text

Summary text refers to putting the main idea and points of the text from the originator in your own words.

Rebecca Moore Howard, an English professor at Syracuse University, has completed extensive research on plagiarism. She has coined a phrase, "patch-writing," which refers to deleting or replacing a few words within a sentence, retaining the originator's sentence structure ("Citation Project"). Patchwriting is problematic because writers do not change the style or content of the originating text, and they do not use quotation marks because they are not directly quoting the originator's text. The result is that the writer's expression does not exist. Therefore, patchwriting is unacceptable. Here are examples of patchwriting:

Original Text from the Journal of Business Ethics by Hansson & Modin

Food risk issues are often scientifically controversial. Assessments of risk are largely based on indirect evidence such as animal data.

Patched Texts

Food risk concerns are often scientifically controversial. Assessments of risk are substantially based on indirect evidence such as animal testing data (Hansson & Modin).

Issues pertaining to food risk concerns are often scientifically controversial. Evaluation of risk are largely based on indirect proof such as animal data (Hansson & Modin).

References

Hansson, S. O. & Modin, P. G. (2011). Moral and instrumental norms in food risk communication. *Journal of Business Ethics, 101(2)*, 313–324. Retrieved from http://ezproxy.hacc.edu/login?url=http://search.ebscohost.com/login.aspx ?direct=true&db=ssf&AN=62001495&site=ehost-live

Closely examine the patched text examples. As you can see, with the exception of a few different words, the sentences are intact. Even though the writing includes an in-text citation and an entry on the documentation page, and both are cited correctly, the writer is still guilty of academic dishonesty, specifically, plagiarism, because one of the three acceptable forms of source incorporation is not used and the originator's concept was not altered enough to distinguish it from the writer.

When writers commit patchwriting, they are compiling, not writing. Franciscan Saint Bonaventura commented on bookmaking and the issues of intellectual property.

Even during the thirteenth century, the discussion of patchwriting, paraphrasing, quoting, and summarizing were part of the public discourse.

A man may write the works of others, adding and changing nothing, in which case he is simply called a scriptor (scribe). Another writes the works of others with additions which are not his own; and he is called a compilator (compiler). Another writes both others' work and his own, but the others' work in principal place, adding his own for purposes of explanation; and he is called a commentator, not an "author." Another writes both his own work and others', but with his own work in principal place, adding others' for purposes of confirmation; and such a man should be called an auctor (author) (Burrow 615).

By today's standards, Saint Bonaventura's words illustrate the point vividly: to avoid plagiarism, it is important for you to understand the choices, both acceptable and unacceptable, for writing with integrity.

Two criteria are necessary to ensure proper attribution in academic and professional writing: citation and documentation. Your writing must include both.

Sam Eshaghoff took the SAT and ACT many times, but not because his scores were low. On the contrary, he was so proficient that he hired himself out to take the exams for others. For this misrepresentation and imper-sonation, he was paid as much as $2,500 per test. His cheating scheme was so organized that the Nassau County (New York) district attorney labeled him as the "academic gun for hire." (60 Minutes).

Mr. Eshaghoff was very orga-nized and egregious in his cheat-ing. He really did not suffer any consequences.

Do you agree? What punish-ment should he have received?

To view the interview, visit http://www.cbsnews.com/8301-18560_162-57348498/the-per-fect-score-cheating-on-the-sat/

Works Cited

Eshaghoff, Sam. Interview with Allison Stewart. "The Perfect Score: Cheating on the SAT. CBS News. 60 Minutes, 1 Jan. 2012. Web, 18 Apr. 2012.

Citation refers to acknowledging a source within the text (also known as in-text citation). A citation immediately follows text that has been quoted, paraphrased, or summarized. A citation for each quote, paraphrase, and summary is important because it signals the reader that the information is source generated. The citation leads the reader to the documentation page, which contains detailed information about the citation to assist the reader in finding additional information about the cited work.

If you are a student of a particular age, you may remember using footnotes to document citations. A superscript number would appear at the end of a sentence that was quoted or paraphrased. At the end of that page, a line was typed across the page. Under the line, the documentation for the citation would appear. If you carry this same style to an academic paper today, your instructor would probably fail the paper because this is an antiquated way to cite for MLA and APA. You may ask why you would fail the paper; after all, you cited the information. You must remember that standards of citation dictate that you use a current acceptable style for academic papers.

Here are examples of how to present an in-text citation for MLA and APA format. Note: A signal phrase is an introduction to a source's information. Your writing comes through via signal phrases and through your analysis and interpretation.

MLA Citation from Scholarly Journal, Paraphrase, Without Signal Phrase:

African art historians face many issues when they record African history (Peffer 70).

MLA Citation from Scholarly Journal, Paraphrase, With Signal Phrase:

According to art history scholar John Peffer, African art historians face many issues when they record African history (70).

APA Citation from Scholarly Journal, Paraphrase, Without Signal Phrase:

African art historians face many issues when they record African history (Peffer, 2005, p. 70).

APA Citation from Scholarly Journal, Paraphrase, With Signal Phrase:

According to art history scholar John Peffer, African art historians face many issues when they record African history (2005, p. 70).

Documentation refers to the bibliographic page, known as Works Cited for MLA (Modern Language Association) format or References for APA (American Psychology Association) format. Documentation includes the source information in its entirety (publisher, author, editor, web name, etc.). More information about MLA and APA appears throughout the textbook.

MLA Works Cited

Peffer, John. "Notes on African Art, History, and Diasporas Within." *African Arts* 38:4 (2005): 70–77, 95–96. *ProQuest*. Web. 2 Feb. 2012.

APA References

Peffer, J. (2005). Notes on African art, history, and diasporas within. *African Arts, 38(4)*, 70–77, 95–96. Retrieved from http://ezproxy.hacc.edu/login?url=http://search.proquest.com/docview/220979100?accountid=11302

As you can see, each citation and documentation style has its own format. The key to academic honesty is using the correct format.

> Honest Reflection: What will I do to ensure I am citing and documenting correctly? Describe specific solutions.

Another proponent to avoid academic dishonesty is to become informed. You must read and research your topic to make informed decisions about what the text means and what the text implies to you. These are the marks of critical thinking and reading. The evidence and the opinions you form must be sound for you to synthesize information. Synthesizing refers to combining different ideas and facts to form a new single idea. Synthesizing helps you to compose a report instead of compiling information from various sources.

As you read, examine how terms are presented; look at both the connotation and denotation of words. Connotation is the personal definition of a word. Connotation, therefore, is subjective. Denotation is a concrete definition of the word. Denotation is often called dictionary meaning; therefore, it is objective. To ensure that all readers understand your synthesis and meaning, your goal is to denote meaning as opposed to connoting meaning.

You must use reliable sources to capsulate the source data you want to present in your writing. Using unreliable sources decreases your credibility. The following chapter explains how to locate and incorporate reliable sources in your writing.

Works Cited

Burrow, John. *The Medieval Compendium*. Times Literary Supplement. 21 May 1976. Print.

Brown, Jeffrey. Transcript of Interview with Kaavya Viswanathan. "Publisher Pulls Harvard Student's Novel Over Alleged Plagiarism." PBS Newshour, 2 May 2006. Web. 19 Apr. 2012.

Dempsey, Judy. "Plagiarism in Dissertation Costs German Defense Minister His Job." *The New York Times* 2 Mar. 2011, late ed., sec. A0. Web.

Eisenstein, Elizabeth L. *The Printing Revolution in Early Modern Europe*. New York: Cambridge University Press, 2005. Print.

Leitch, Vincent B., ed. *The Norton Anthology of Theory and Criticism*. 1st ed. New York: W. W. Norton & Company, Inc., 2001. 1617. Print.

Moore, Rebecca Howard. *The Citation Project*, n.d. Web. 17 Apr. 2012. <http://site.citationproject.net/>.

"Plagiarism." *Chambers Dictionary of Etymology*. 1988. Print.

"Plagiarism." *Issues & Controversies*. Facts On File News Services, 18 Oct. 2010. Web. 15 Jan. 2012.

"Royal Society." *History*. Excellence in Science, n.d. Web. 17 Apr. 2012.<http://royalsociety.org/about-us/history/>.

Stolberg, Sheryl Gay. "Bush Aide Resigns Over Plagiarism in Columns He Wrote." *The New York Times* 1 Mar. 2008, late ed., sec. A0. Web.

Rate Your Academic Honesty IQ—Posttest

Complete the following posttest. Note: Do not refer to the answers given on the pretest (remember academic honesty).

What is plagiarism?
When you were first introduced to the term plagiarism?
What did you learn about plagiarism?
Check the statements regarding plagiarism that you think are true.
_____ If 50% or more of a paper is from sources and I correctly cite and document the sources, I have not committed plagiarism.
_____ If 25% or more of a paper is from sources and I correctly cite and document the sources, I have not committed plagiarism.

_____ I can write a paper for one class and submit the same paper (or with minor modification) for another class.

_____ Students commit plagiarism because they do not know what it is.

_____ Students commit plagiarism because they do not think they will get caught.

_____ Students commit plagiarism because they do not care about the ramifications.

_____ Students commit plagiarism because they do not have time to write the paper.

_____ Students who give or receive answers for any assignment or use devices or documents prohibited by the instructor are committing plagiarism.

_____ Students who falsify documents to take an examine for someone else are committing plagiarism.

_____ Students who use and/or submit the work of another as their own are committing plagiarism.

_____ Students who buy or sell essays, research papers, assignments, laboratory assignments, computer programs, or any class-related information are committing plagiarism.

_____ Students falsifying their own or another's academic records, or falsifying of admissions, registration, or other related college materials are committing plagiarism.

CHAPTER 2

Research to Incorporate Reliable Sources

You may choose a variety of sources, from open source to peer reviewed. Regardless of the source, you must apply a reliability spectrum test to each source you use. This chapter provides tips and techniques to ensure that you understand how to incorporate reliable sources in your writing by:

- Avoiding plagiarism
- Conducting research
- Synthesizing information
- Determining how to use the cited information
- Building credibility
- Supporting a position

Often, students will state that they do not know the subject; therefore, they cannot add to the discussion. Instead, they will write a compilation paper—a paper that strings together quotes, summaries, paraphrasing, and "patchwriting" to express information. Even if students properly cite sources, the paper is considered to be plagiarized. Why? Because the student did not write the paper. You may have asked yourself these questions as you have completed initial research:

- How can you write a paper and incorporate reliable sources?
- How can you write a paper and incorporate sources when you are not the expert?
- What is wrong with submitting the same paper for two different classes? The paper is cited and documented correctly, and I did not compile sources.

This chapter provides concrete tips to help you complete the process.

Chapter Objectives

After reading this chapter and completing the exercises, you will be able to:

- Differentiate between reliable and unreliable sources.
- Assess the content within a source.
- Analyze the ethical choices writers face.

Avoiding Plagiarism

Cases of academic dishonesty are reported to be on the rise. The results of the 2003 National Survey of Student Engagement highlighted the fact that students reported their peers copying information from the internet without citing the source 87% of the time (U. C. Academic Integrity). Are these results similar to your responses on the pretest and posttest? Students cite several reasons for committing academic dishonesty: lack of time, belief that they will not get caught, lack of interest, belief that no thought is original.

Why is plagiarism such a serious offense? Why do so many students think it is acceptable?

Many students do not view academic dishonesty as an offense because they believe no thought is original, that all thoughts are influenced by someone else. However, everyone has opinions and information to share. You have a perspective that you can expound, and you can support or negate an opposing point of view with reliable sources.

Let us examine the questions posed on Test Your Academic Honesty IQ. Highlighted are the reasons why academic dishonesty, not honesty, is being committed.

Check the statements regarding plagiarism that you think are true.	
_____ If 50% or more of a paper is from sources and I correctly cite and document the sources, I have not committed plagiarism.	False. Fifty percent, even if cited and documented correctly, constitutes a compilation paper.
_____ If 25% or more of a paper is from sources and I correctly cite and document the sources, I have not committed plagiarism.	False. Strive for 75% of the writing. Correctly document and cite the 25% of sources used.
_____ I can write a paper for one class and submit the same paper (or with minor modification) for another class.	Professors expect you to write one paper per assignment, regardless of the course. Fair use laws determine the percentage of sources that are allowable for a document. Fair use in the college classroom dictates that you write a paper for a specific class. Making alterations most likely not produce a positive outcome because the audience and expectations are different.

———— Students who give or receive answers for any assignment or use devices or documents prohibited by the instructor are committing plagiarism.	Yes. If the offense involves writing, it is plagiarism. Otherwise, it is outright the academic dishonesty offense of cheating. For example, texting answers, using a calculator, passing notes, copying and distributing a test or assignment.
———— Students who falsify documents to take an examine for someone else are committing plagiarism.	Yes. Any falsification results in academic dishonesty. For example, completing assignments and tests for an on-line student; registering as a student and taking an exam for some else.
———— Students who use and/or submit the work of another as their own are committing plagiarism.	Yes. Any falsification results in academic dishonesty. For example, a friend or family member completing an assignment for you.
———— Students who buy or sell essays, research papers, assignments, laboratory assignments, computer programs, or any class-related information are committing plagiarism.	Yes. Any falsification results in academic dishonesty.
———— Students falsifying their own or another's academic records, or falsifying of admissions, registration, or other related college materials are committing plagiarism.	Yes. Any falsification results in academic dishonesty.

Ethical Principles Applicable to Writing

There are best practices that you can implement to ensure that your writing is correct, thoughtful, thorough, readable, and understandable. In their simplistic form, ethical principles are writing that projects its subject rightly or wrongly. Two categories of unethical writing are sin of commission and sin of omission.

Commission refers to completing a job someone requests, in other words, an assignment. For example, your professor or supervisor has asked you to write a research paper describing how companies use social media to increase sales. The information will be used to recommend whether a particular business should use social media. Here is the business profile:

- Four-year-old jewelry retail business, specializing in sterling silver and gemstones jewelry for men and women
- Owner designs and makes all jewelry
- Owner has three employees
- Customers age average is 42
- Owner has gained 20% profit over the past four years
- Owner wants you to write a business plan that explains the advantages and disadvantages of using social media for a small, upstart business.

> Ethical Reflection: What will you do when you cannot find sources on your topic or when you cannot find sources to support your opinion?

You discover that it is difficult to find scholarly support for this niche market. Instead of presenting your findings accurately, you decide to present it using sins of commission. Let us say that you are of the opinion that the business should not use social media. You have searched business databases such as Business ProQuest and Business Source Premier. However, you are not finding data that support your position. In addition to being plagiarism, manipulating or changing information is a sin of commission. Although the citation and documentation are formatted correctly, you have submitted a sin of commission because you changed the outcome of the source's data.

Sin of omission refers to deliberately or unintentionally excluding data. For example, not including negative issues pertaining to a topic or not thoroughly explaining the cause of something and how other factors are influenced by the cause are sins of are included in the table below.

What Would You Do If ...

Throughout your academic and professional careers, you will be faced with ethical decisions; some will be more serious than others. However, each will entail making the best judgment for your future.

The International Center for Academic Integrity, sponsored by Clemson University, has published case studies on its website to help students and professionals determine the best course of action for various academic integrity scenarios. What would you do? How far are you willing to go if placed in various academic dilemmas? Visit http://www.academicintegrity.org/educational_resources/educational_materials/casestudies.php to read and respond to the case studies.

Sins of Commission	Sins of Omission
Using three-dimensional visuals to focus the reader's attention on one area instead of the entire visual	Eliminating negative effects of new safety procedure
Changing photographs to manipulate the impact of the nonverbal data	Suppressing ingredients and formulas
Lying about the completion of primary research	Suppressing evidence
Plagiarizing	Eliminating citations and documentation

Other Other examples of sins of commission and omission are included in the table above:

There are ten tips in the section "Conducting Research" that will help you to refrain from committing sins of omission and commission.

Conducting Research

Research writing involves the convergence of strategies to aid you in composing writer-generated texts. This section provides you with several tips to help you complete the writing process. Think of researching as an opportunity to discover information.

Tip One—Time Management

Researching and writing take time; therefore, you want to avoid procrastination. Although you may think that you write your best under pressure, you need time to conduct research and verify sources. It is possible that your idea will not garnish enough information. You may have to alter or totally change your approach. Time management is important because you must complete several validity test steps.

Here are some suggestions that may help you to manage your time effectively:

- Write a project to-do list, beginning with the project due date. Working from the due date backward works well because the deadline is prominent in your mind. Be sure to include the steps of the writing process; otherwise, you will defeat the purpose of the project to-do list.

- Plan chunks of time per day for each assignment until the due date, if you are working on multiple assignments.
- Allow for unforeseen circumstances that may occur, such as added hours to your work schedule, illness, or family obligations.

Complete the following chart by describing specific actions you will take to manage your time.

How will I manage my time to ensure I am doing everything I can do to management my time in a way to be cognizant of academic honesty?

_____

_____

_____

Tip Two—Assignment Topic

When you brainstorm topics, you will probably have broad subjects in mind. A subject will uncover literally hundreds, if not thousands, of resources.

How can you possibly scan all of the sources? Well, you cannot. However, perhaps by looking at the titles and reading the abstracts, you can narrow your search. Try it.

Search an electronic database available to you via your campus library. An electronic database stores articles from a variety of sources for easy access to researchers. Type search words pertaining to your topic for easy retrieval of related documents. To focus your search further, be sure to locate the peer-reviewed box. Click on the box to receive articles that experts in the field have

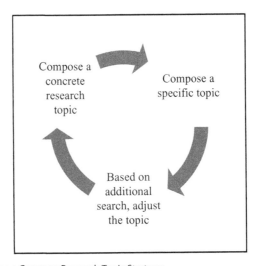

Compose a concrete research topic

Compose a specific topic

Based on additional search, adjust the topic

Figure 2.1 Developing a Concrete Research Topic Strategy

edited and reviewed. For this topic, try EbsoHost (search databases with every academic/discipline area), ProQuest (search for scholarly articles from journals, magazines, and newspapers), or ARTstor (search a collection of images). Search the broad topic "African Art." Based on the results, formulate a searchable, narrow persuasive topic on African art. Determine what it is about African art that you want to examine. What position do you want to pursue? Figure 2.1 helps you to visualize how you want to think about search parameters.

Note: You may have to conduct a second- or third-level search to further narrow the topic to ensure it is manageable and relevant.

Tip Three—Usability of a Source

You will want to use several criteria to measure whether a source will help you develop your position, particularly for internet sources.

Writing style: Look for sources that are content relevant, meaning that the sources are well developed, contain an extensive source list, present multiple perspectives (are not one-sided), and are bias-free (the information does not have a particular slant or agenda).

Format: Look for information that appears in fine print. Is the author hiding information (sin of commission)? Does the source contain advertisements? This issue is of particular concern for web pages. Examine the advertisers or sponsors. What products are they pushing? Are there any hidden agendas? Even if you are required to use URLs ending in .org, .gov, or .edu, you still must examine these points.

Follow the Link/Source Within a Website

For each web page that you want to use as a source, complete the following checklist.

Verification Category	Verification Details
Sponsor(s)	
Author(s) To verify authenticity	
Authors' credentials	
Affiliations	
Date	
Evidence of bias	
Evidence of objectivity	

Verification Category	Verification Details
Links	
Rhetorical purpose	

When conducting a search on a search engine such as Google, why do you want to stay away from the first four listings? Identify at least two reasons.

Tip Four—Document as You Go

Have you ever recorded a quote or summarized a paragraph but neglected to write down the page number, publisher, or any other necessary source information? Nothing can be more frustrating than wasting time by re-searching when you are in the thralls of writing the paper. Get in the routine of taking notes and recording source information so that you cover all aspects of the writing process accurately and timely. Refer to the chapter supplemental information for a source checklist to help you with documenting as you go.

Even if you are unsure about whether you will use a source, if you are thinking about it, record the source information. If you find an electronic copy of a source in your college library database, you can usually e-mail the article to yourself. When you do so, the source documenting information usually appears; be sure to verify that it does. Once you have the file, you can highlight the portion that you want to quote, summarize, or paraphrase. Save the article to your flash drive. Be sure to create a file that contains only files for a particular paper. This system will ensure that all of your sources are together. Also, you can check the source with your paraphrase and summary to ensure that it reflects your writing and is not plagiarized.

Avoid cutting and pasting the portion of the originator's text into your draft. Separate your work from the originator's work so that you will not be tempted to replace a few of the originator's words. Read the article, and jot down the premise in your own words on paper; or read the article, close the file, open your draft, and summarize or paraphrase the information. Compare your version to the originator's version. Did you reflect the main idea in your own words? If so, continue with writing signal phrases and adding additional information. If not, try again. Also, consider whether the source is relevant to your topic.

For web pages, capture a screen print of the site or print the site's page. If you capture information from a link that appears on the site, be sure to record the URL (universal resource locator) of the originating page. Recording the URL is important to keep track of all sponsoring sites. You may determine that the links are not reliable or the sponsors may have an agenda that, on the surface, is not apparent.

If you prefer to work with hard copies, copy the page of the source you plan to quote, paraphrase, or summarize. Copy the information for documenting the source. Read the portion that you plan to use. Put the source away, and place the paraphrase or summary in your own words. Compare the source with your summary or paraphrase. Is it too close to the originator's source? If so, try again. Keep all the information for this particular paper in a folder.

Determining whether an article is reliable and appropriate for your paper: Read the abstract of a paper to determine an article's subject without reading or scanning the entire article. However, you do not want to paraphrase or summarize an article based on its abstract because, by their nature, abstracts are summaries of the article. It is meaningless to summarize a summary. It is impossible to write an abstract that reflects your ideas. Let's take a closer look. Here is the abstract for the article "Moral and Instrumental Norms in Food Risk Communication." You will work with excerpts of this article throughout the textbook.

The major normative recommendations in the literature on food risk communication can be summarized in the form of seven practical principles for such communication: (1) Be honest and open. (2) Disclose incentives and conflicts of interest. (3) Take all available relevant knowledge into consideration. (4) When possible, quantify risks. (5) Describe and explain uncertainties. (6) Take all the publics' concerns into account. (7) Take the rights of individuals and groups seriously. We show that each of these proposed principles can be justified both in terms of more fundamental ethical principles and instrumentally in terms of the communicating agent's self-interest. The mechanisms of this concordance of justifications are discussed. It is argued that the concordance is specific for areas such as food risks in which agents such as companies and public authorities are highly dependent on the public's trust and confidence. The implications of these findings both for moral philosophy and for practical food risk communication are discussed (Modin and Hansson).

Springer Science & Business Media. Journal of Business Ethics, Vol. 101, No. 2, 2011, pp. 313-324. Peter G. Modin and Sven Ove Hansson. Reprinted with kind permission from Springer Science and Business Media.

It is difficult to condense this abstract any further without plagiarizing its content.

Tip Five—Represent the Source Accurately

If you quote only a portion of a sentence, you must include ellipses to indicate that words are missing from the quote. The goal of using ellipses is to tighten the language of a quote. Include the ellipses (three periods in the text) when you delete words to emphasize a point. Be very careful with using ellipses. If you drop words for the purpose of manipulating the information to support your position, you are committing both sins of omission and commission. This unethical writing style lessens your credibility and position.

Here is an example of an acceptable use of the ellipses.
Original: "Art, in the same way, posits man's physical and spiritual existence, but in none of its works is it concerned with his response" (Arendt 69).
With ellipses: "Art ... posits man's physical and spiritual existence, but in none of its works is it concerned with his response" (Arendt 69).

Works Cited

Arendt, Hannah, ed. Illuminations Walter Benjamin Essays and Reflections. New York: Harcourt, Brace &World, 1968. Print.

Taking the phrase "in the same way" out of the sentence does not alter the meaning, because the focus of the quote is Walter Benjamin's view of the response of connoisseur of art, which is less important than his feeling and presence with the art.

Application: Include ellipses in the following quote. Your goal is to keep the original intent of the text by eliminating unnecessary words. Be sure to include the in-text citation.

Researchers do not only describe and analyze the communication activities of companies and authorities. More often than not, they also turn normative and comment on what was right and—in particular—on what went wrong in these activities (Hansson and Modin 314).

Placement of In-Text Citation

Many students struggle with where in the sentence they should place an in-text citation. Placement of an in-text citation for a quote is straightforward: the citation appears after the quotation. The place of a citation for a summary or paraphrase is not so straightforward, especially when you incorporate your writing with a lead-in phrase or a lead-out phrase. Where does it go in relation to a summary or paraphrase? How will your instructor know where your words end and a summary or paraphrase begins? The best method to follow is to organize the message to make clear distinctions between your writing and the sources' writing. Single phrases and transitional phrases, such as those explaining the author's credentials, help to make the distinction. You do not want to summarize or paraphrase a huge chunk of text. Remember the distinct purpose for a quote, a paraphrase, and a summary. Here is an example:

Original Text

Proper attribution of sources and the related academic integrity guidelines are often covered in required high-school and college English classes, and additional assistance is often available to students through a writing center. Although plagiarism is probably almost as old as communication itself, the internet and other information technologies (IT) have made it easier to commit and harder to detect. Resent years have seen a growing discussion and body of literature on the effects of the internet and other information technologies on plagiarism (Gomez, 2001; Bugeja, 2000) (215).

Source: Nitterhouse, Denise. Plagiarism—Not Just An "Academic" Problem. Teaching Business Ethics 7: 215–27, 2005

Sources acknowledged within the article:

Gomez, D. S.: 2001, "It's Just So Easy To Cheat," *NEA Today*, April 19(7), p. 42.

Bugeja, M.: 2000, "Confronting the New Breed of Plagiarist: Stealing with the Aid of a Computer," *Editor & Publisher*, the Fourth Estate (March 20) 133(12), p. 46.

Paraphrase and Writer's Commentary?

For each sentence, label whether it is a summary, a quote, a paraphrase, or writer's commentary. Writer's commentary is how to move from your writing to incorporating a source.

The discussion of plagiarism usually starts in the English classroom; however, the conversation must not end there. The internet and other technology make it easier to copy information from various sources, but harder to detect. Therefore, the conversation on academic and profession honesty should take place across all disciplines.

Rewrite the paragraph to strengthen it and correctly incorporate in-text citations.

Using Brackets Within a Quote

The value of a quote may be high in some cases; however, a word may need clarification or to be put into context for the reader. To improve the readability of the quote, it may be best to place information that needs to be clarified or defined in brackets. Think of the use of brackets as meaning "in other words." Bracket words when you would rather keep as much of the originator's words as possible; paraphrasing would not have such a powerful impact as just clarifying a word. Just as ellipses do, brackets tighten the quote.

Example:

In the utilitarian tradition [morality for the greater good of society], lying is not universally prohibited, but has to be judged according to the moral value of its consequences. However, utilitarians have been eager to show that untruthfulness has so bad consequences that it is very seldom justified (Modin and Hansson 317).

It is possible to use ellipses and brackets in the same quote. However, be very careful. Psychologically, information that contains more than one ellipsis and set of brackets suggests that perhaps the source is not as reliable as it should be.

Using *Sic* to Represent the Originator's Character

When using an originator's words that are, for example, ungrammatical, contain a double-entendre, or include an incorrect fact, you can write "(sic)" next to the word. This alerts the reader that this is the correct quote. In what circumstances would you use sic instead of brackets with the correct word?

- When you want to capture the emotion of the originator's words
- When you want to capture the attitude projected in the originator's words
- When the originator's words are unique

Common Knowledge

To cite or not to cite; that is the question. Is this adaptation of Shakespeare's soliloquy plagiarism? You must cite and document information, research, data, concepts, and ideas that are quoted, paraphrased, or summarized.

What are other reasons for using sic?

However, information that is well known, easily verifiable, and easily accessible needs no citation or documentation. This information includes historical facts and calculations. Here are a few examples:

- There are approximately 300 million American citizens.
- Barak Obama was elected president of the United States in 2008.
- AIDS refers to autoimmune deficiency syndrome.

Think of common knowledge as historical tidbits that are part of public discourse and public knowledge; the information cannot be disputed. Should you be unsure about whether information is common knowledge, you can check multiple sources to determine whether the information is easily accessible. If you cannot determine, when it doubt, cite the source.

List three academic, historical, or social phrases that you think are common knowledge.

1.

2.

3.

Tip Six—Represent Your Writing Accurately

Remember that you are not a complier of information; you are the writer. Therefore, your writing must have prominence. You may use numerous writing techniques to tap into your critical thinking and writing skills. When you use critical thinking and writing skills, you are analyzing to evaluate what a text means, and explaining and connecting its meaning to areas within the scope of your topic. To critically think about a subject, you must determine what you currently know about the subject.

What do you know? Your mind is filled with data that include, but certainly are not limited to historical or obscure references (popular culture references), prose, clichés, historical events, or mathematical calculations. Making logical connections among data can help you expound on new or emerging information. To help you incorporate your ideas and to clarify information to an academic or professional audience, you can incorporate allusions. Allusions are references to something or someone that are used to clarify a point or make a point vivid. One concern when writing allusions is that your audience may not understand the reference; thus, the audience may not understand your points.

Write an allusive statement for each of the following topics. Do not research the topic. Formulate your statement based on you current knowledge.

1. The collapse of the banking industry

2. The debate of the effectiveness of drugs for patients who are diagnosed with depression

3. The privacy issues pertaining to internet searches

You have seen the term *signal phrase* used a few times in your textbook. You compose signal phrases to explain source information using supporting details that develop your main ideas. A signal phrase introduces an originator's text, regardless of whether it is a paraphrase, quote, or summary. Signal phrases can serve as transitions phrases that link a source with your position and the position of the paper. They can explain the significance of a source to the context of your paper, define terms, expand your main ideas, and explain what a source is saying by putting information in context. This means providing information about the source, explaining any affiliations the source may have, and identifying any biases that are apparent. Note: You can write more than one signal sentence to lead to the originator's text. Do not include perfunctory information for signal phrases.

Academic Vocabulary

You want to project a certain cadence as you paraphrase, summarize, and explain information. Putting information in your own words does not mean it is acceptable to use your everyday, slang, and conversational language. Your instructor expects you to show your sophistication with academic language and writing. Your writing must be specific to concrete instead of vague to abstract. You do not want to use empty words—words that do not add meaning to your sentence—just for the sake of filling a page. Nor do you want to use hyperbolic words.

Here are some words and phrases that are not acceptable as academic or professional. For each vague and abstract choice, write a corresponding academic and professional choice. Add the appropriate details to support your academic and professional choice.

Conversational Option—Vague and Abstract Choice	Academic Option—Academic and Professional Choice
a lot	
who, which, that, there	
reached a decision	
we here at/here at	
few	
in order to	
quantity	
due to the fact that the majority point of view	
at this point in time	
very	
in the near future	
a good number of	
most of the people (employees, researchers, authors, etc.)	
past experience	
many	

A thesaurus is beneficial in helping you expand your vocabulary. However, do not use it as an excuse to commit plagiarism, for example, by using a thesaurus to change words in a sentence but keep the originator's sentence structure (refer to patchwriting).

> **Avoiding Plagiarism Alert**: Using synonyms does not prevent you from committing plagiarism. If you capture the originator's idea, concept, or thought using different words, you have committed plagiarism. You must significantly change the wording *and* cite the source.

Verbs are phrased in the active and passive voice. The active voice pertains to the subject of sentence performing the action. Passive voice refers to de-emphasizing the activity of the subject. For example:

The results of the archaeological exhibition conducted by Dr. McPherson were reported on the "Anthropological Studies Center" website. (Passive voice)

Dr. McPherson conducted an archaeological exhibition to Cairo, Egypt. His results are posted on the "Anthropological Studies Center" website. (Active voice)

An archaeological exhibition to Cairo, Egypt, was conducted by Dr. McPherson. The results can be found in the "Anthropological Studies Center" website. (Passive voice)

Phrasing your text in the active voice will help the reader understand your structure and organization better because your writing is tighter and the meaning is stronger. You should use an expository, third-person voice throughout the paper. Report writing uses the imperative, which means active verbs are presented in a command or instructional voice.

You can use the following list of verbs to compose paraphrases, summaries, and signal phrases. Some verbs are stronger than others in both meaning and impact. Place a check in the box of each verb you believed to be strong.

Table 2.1 Writing Style—Strong Verb

	Strong Verbs	Weak Verbs
Recommend		
Implied		
Explained		
Signified		
Decided		

Decoded		
Believed		
Said		
Stated		
Suggested		
Observed		
Understand		
Argued		
Assumed		
Reasoned		
Concluded		
Demonstrated		
Learned		
Conducted		
Implement		
Taught		
Define		

Tip Seven—Build Credibility

Philosophers Aristotle and Plato built their arguments through ethos, pathos, and logos. These persuasive appeals are at the heart of building credibility. Ethos refers to how credible is the information you provide. This credibility pertains to both your writing and the sources that you use. Your credibility is as strong as your writing. Pathos refers to the emotion of the descriptive language you use. Logos refers to the logic you use to support your points. Various levels of sources are available, from open sources to peer-reviewed sources.

Ethos, pathos, and logos can cancel each other. For example, you can write a research paper that is factual and interspersed with an emotional appeal, but is supported with subjective prose rather than facts. The prose manipulates the reader with emotions instead of logic. When this happens, you lose ethos.

The strength of the paper falls on the credibility of its secondary resources, which refer to research conducted by authors, researchers, and scientists. The most reliable secondary sources are peer reviewed. These articles are called scholarly articles.

For internet searches, begin by searching the websites with the extensions .org, .gov, and .edu. Although you cannot always count on the validity of any website, these sites are a good starting point. Where does the source originate? If you cannot determine the publisher for an internet source after the second page, consider not using it. Reliable sources will publish their name on the first screen. Who is the sponsor of the site? You should be able to determine the sponsor on the first page, as well. The sponsor should present the information neutrally, without providing a slant or taking a concrete position. The information should provide the pro and con aspects of the topic. What is the date? Reliable sources will update the site monthly, not yearly. Are the credentials of the writers and editors listed? What links are provided? If the site provides links, are those links reliable? Is the URL to that link distinct, or is the URL linked to the sponsoring site?

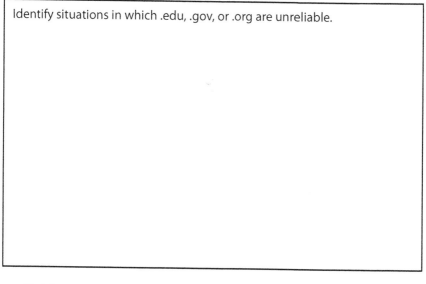

Identify situations in which .edu, .gov, or .org are unreliable.

Databases you can access at your college or workplace are more reliable and easier to use. Articles on databases such as EbsoHost© and Lexus Nexus© have been peer edited. The following screen print captures the searchable EbsoHost screen indicating the location of the peer review check box. By checking the box, you will only receive peer-reviewed articles pertaining to your subject.

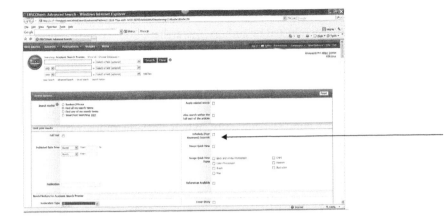

These databases contain academic journals that you should use to emphasize the fact that research in academia and business supports your arguments.

Many students are tempted to use popular magazines because they are easily accessible and a common reading source for students. These magazines are a part of pop culture. For a variety of reasons, many professors will not allow popular magazines as a reliable source or a source you should include to validate your arguments. One reason is because these magazines rarely provide the writer's credentials and source list. Exceptions often are *Time* or *Newsweek*.

Newspapers such as *The New York Times* and *The Wall Street Journal* are generally accepted as reliable, even though they rarely give detailed source information. The reputation of the newspapers results in the credibility of its reporters.

Since the passage of the first amendment to the Constitution, freedom of the press, journalists have understood the importance of confirming data because, depending on the topic, they are not obligated to reveal sources.

The first amendment to the U.S. Constitution states:

> Congress shall make no law respecting an establishment of religion, or prohibiting the free exercise thereof; or abridging the freedom of speech, or of the press; or the right of the people peaceably to assemble, and to petition the government for a redress of grievances.

This freedom is not carte blanche; reporters can be found in contempt if, for example, a judge orders them to reveal their sources, but they refuse in an effort to uphold the integrity of the profession or protect a source. Of course, this freedom does not mean that journalist are allowed to falsify information because they believe they won't get caught. When one high-profile case of journalistic improprieties occurs, the public disdain for journalism increases a notch. The first amendment does not give journalists the right to publish false information. The Society of Professional Journalists upholds the ethical standards of the profession.

Tip Eight—Write a Concise Thesis Statement

A statement of purpose is necessary for any written document. For essays, this statement is known as a thesis statement—a sentence or two that concisely identify the topic and main point of a piece of writing. Contained within the paragraph of the thesis is information to support it. This information includes contextual data such as background, areas the essay will investigate, and the purpose for the essay. This paragraph is powerful because it supports the entire essay; all of your writing must provide details to support this paragraph. The body of the report contains details to support your thesis. When drafting the paper, make sure each paragraph focuses on an idea of your own, with the support for the idea coming from your sources. A thesis statement is a building block in writing because it helps you focus your writing. How can a thesis statement help you to showcase your writing?

A strong thesis will result in the opportunity for you to write a clear, concise, and writer-driven essay. Should you experience trouble composing your thesis, you may have to learn more about the subject by analyzing and reading critically, or change the focus of the paper. An underdeveloped thesis statement can lead to anxiety and the temptation to use more source information than is acceptable.

> Application: Write a thesis statement for any subject of choice. Find a source from an academic journal, one source from a popular magazine, and one source from a newspaper. Write a two-page compare-and-contrast paper explaining how each source treats the subject. Explain how each is reliable, unreliable, answers questions you may have, etc.

Tip Nine—Conduct Primary Research

You can become a source by conducting primary research. Primary research involves the writer conducting interviews, surveys, and questionnaires; sharing observations; and testing protocols (testing the validity of an outcome). The advantage to primary research is you can determine the information you need to help you add to the scholarship of the topic. Perhaps there is information that you want to know; however, no resources or not enough resources exist for you to conduct a proper investigation. To explore these untapped areas, critical thinking skills are needed.

Interviews

You should choose an expert in the field who is knowledgeable about your subject. For example, if you are writing a report on why students are not adjusting to the rigors of college math, you should interview high school teachers and college math instructors. Why? Because to want to get various points of view. What questions do you think are important? You do not want to regurgitate information.

Verify with the interviewee that you may use her/his information in the report. To strengthen credibility, you do not want to agree to withhold the person's name in the body. Also, keep the possibility of future correspondence on this topic with the interview, because you may need to clarify information or your reader may want to contact the interviewee to follow up or ask for clarification.

Compose open questions for interviews. Open questions provide the interviewee the opportunity to explain answers in detail. When you begin a question with how, what, why, where, when, or who, you will write an open question. Go into the interview with a set of questions. You should have at least six concrete questions that you want to ask. Be flexible to follow where the interviewee takes you. Remember to ask questions that counter the interviewee's point of view. Doing so will balance the essay and demonstrate that you are thinking about and considering various points of view. The interviewee may discuss a point that may be essential to your data collection. Be willing to let the interviewee guide the interview. However, be willing to get the interviewee back on task, if necessary. So that your data are correct, ask the interviewee whether you can tape the interview. Should he/she refuse, you will have to take excellent notes. When you take notes, be sure to accurately record points that you want to quote. Ask the interviewee to repeat information, if necessary. In the report, explain why the interviewee is important to your research. Include the interviewee's credentials. The strength of the logos and ethos of the report depends on the strength of your primary source.

Surveys

Surveys consist of a list of closed questions, which are easy to answer, usually yes or no or limited-choice questions. When you want to measure how a group feels about subsets of a topic, you can survey a group. The group for surveys, known as a sample, are categorized three ways: convenience, judgment, and random samples. Surveys ask the same questions to the sample group. A convenience sample is an audience to which you have direct access. For example, classmates in your technical writing class are a convenience sample because you can access them during your class. A judgment sample is an audience that is familiar with the subject and has experience with the subject; therefore, this audience is reliable in providing educated responses. An example is surveying students at the college dining room to determine whether an organic foods menu is something the college should implement. A random sample is an audience whose knowledge and background you cannot judge because you do not know. However, the topic is important to a general audience. An example is asking adults at the local mall their opinion about nationalized health care.

> **Ethical Reflection**
> There are potential downsides to each sample. What are some you can think of? What are potential problems in the examples above?

How to Interpret and Report Primary Research

Interviews

In the body of the essay, you want to provide information about the interviewee; what credentials does the interviewee have that make him or her an expert in the subject? Provide the interviewee's titles, education, and years of experience in this explanation. The body of the essay should focus on two to four answers that highlight, support, and question your thesis.

> **Ethical Reflection**
> Why is it vital to include the opposing point of view to any report?

Provide an overall summary for the remaining questions. This summary can appear throughout the report where you want to support a point.

Refrain from including a list of questions and answers in the body of the report. Usually, this formatting results in a stagnant presentation of information. You want to present primary research to link your points together; it should serve as a road map for your audience to follow your logical and credibility.

Surveys

In the body of the essay, you want to present the data clearly and neutrally. Provide an overview of your sample group (whether the group was a judgment, convenience, or random sample), why you chose that type of sample, how the knowledge base of the sample supports your thesis, how the knowledge base of the sample does not fit your thesis, etc. Present data in a chart to summarize the results.

The documentation style determines the citation for primary research. For the APA format, primary research does not include a citation. Your lead-in to the data signals primary research.

Example, APA Style

During an interview to discuss business ethics, Business Professor William Ashour stated the most compelling characteristic workers should have is professionalism.

The most compelling characteristic workers should have is professionalism (W. Ashour, personal interview, 2012, Feb. 1).

A notation on the References page does not appear.

Example, MLA Style

In contrast, MLA style requires an in-text citation indicating to the reader that a notation for the interview appears on the documentation page.

During an interview to discuss business ethics, Business Professor William Ashour stated that the most compelling characteristic workers should have is professionalism (Personal interview).

Works Cited

Ashour, William. Personal interview. 22 Feb. 2011.

Note: Personal interview refers to a face-to-face meeting. The entry depends on the type of interview conducted. Telephone interviews or e-mail interviews are acceptable as primary research. Remember to keep all records and notes pertaining to the interview.

Citing Primary Research in APA

As for citing interview and survey information within the report, to cite an interview: include first initial and last name of interviewee, personal communication, and date of interview. Do not include documentation for interviews—do not include them on the References page.

For more information on citing primary research, visit http://library.stkate.edu/pdf/citeAPA.pdf

Personal Communications

Examples of personal communications may include personal or telephone interviews, letters, memos, e-mail messages, chats, or other types of discussion formats. Personal communications are cited in the text of the paper only in APA; because they are not considered recoverable, they are not included in the reference list.

Andrea Alves (personal communication, October 11, 2011) states that incidents of plagiarism at ACBEU Language Institute at Victoria, Bahia, Salvador, Brazil are on the rise.

To document surveys that you distributed:

Your last name, first name. "Title of survey." Survey. Date distributed.

Example:

Jones, Lori. "Survey on Needs for Additional Prescription Drug Benefit." Survey. 9 May 2011.

Summary

> **Ethical Reflection**
> What, specifically, will I do to ensure that I am incorporating my writing?

Even if you do not conduct primary research via questionnaires, survey, interviews, or observations, you are still responsible for providing analyzes. You can do so by providing a contrasting viewpoint, testing the results of data, explaining how the data work to support a theory, explaining how to implement a recommendation, and supplying a relevant application.

Tip Ten—Use Visuals with Purpose

Use visuals to emphasize a point that words cannot stress. Visuals include bar charts, line charts, drawings, and photographs. A picture may speak a thousand words; however, a visual should not replace the words.

Using the correct visual is essential in clearly representing the data. The correct visual type will emphasize meaning.

Visuals are cited basically the same way in all source types. The following schematic illustrates how to cite a visual source in MLA format.

When you design a visual based on your data collection via primary research, you have the opportunity to explain the type of primary research you conducted and its relevance to your topic. This explanation serves as the in-text citation for primary search.

By performing all of these tips, you will build credibility because you will demonstrate that you can synthesize information.

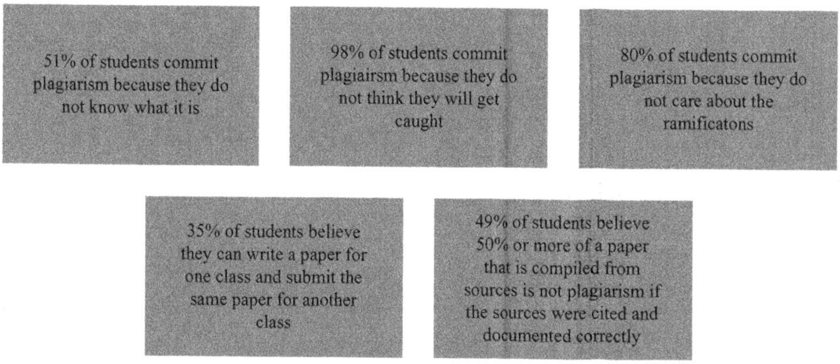

51% of students commit plagiarism because they do not know what it is

98% of students commit plagiarsm because they do not think they will get caught

80% of students commit plagiarism because they do not care about the ramificatons

35% of students believe they can write a paper for one class and submit the same paper for another class

49% of students believe 50% or more of a paper that is compiled from sources is not plagiarism if the sources were cited and documented correctly

Figure 2.2 Student Opinions on Plagiarism (Gray 7)

Works Cited

U. C. Academic Integrity Campaign. Frequently Asked Questions. Sep. 2007. Web. 18 June 2012.

Wang, Jifend, et.al. "The Novel Design and Preliminary Investigation of Composite Material Marine Current Turbine." Chart. *The Archive of Mechanical Engineering* LVIII:4 (2011): 360. Web. 8 June 2012.

Exercises and Application

2.1 To Cite or Not to Cite

For the following cases, determine whether an in-text citation is needed. If so, find the source and write a documentation entry for the source.

Information	To Cite	Not to Cite
The movie *Salmon Fishing In The Yemen* grossed approximately $74,000 on March 11, 2012.		
Rick Santorum won the Kansas Super Tuesday for the Republican presidential primary at 51.2%.		
"One man is as good as another until he has written a book." Benjamin Jowett		
Ask not what your country can do for you; ask what you can do for your country. John F. Kennedy		
According to Amanda Fortini in an article entitled "Special Treatment" At Wonderland Center, a drug rehabilitation facility, the rich and famous live as if they are staying at a luxury hotel. They can take a hiatus from their treatment. Celebrities can use their electronics; actors can continue to work on films and singers can continue to tour.		
Lorraine Hansberry wrote the play, *A Raisin in the Sun*.		

Should you deem it necessary to cite, here are the sources:

http://boxofficemojo.com/daily/chart/ (Box Office Mojo 11 Mar. 2012).

The Oxford Dictionary of Quotations, third edition, 1979. Oxford University Press: New York. (285)

Hansberry, Lorraine. *A Raisin in the Sun*. Signet Book. Penguin Group: New York. 1988.

The New Yorker, Letter from West Hollywood Special Treatment: The rise of luxury rehab. Fortini, Amanda. Pp. 40–47 (41).

At what end of the scale does this situation belong? If it does not need citing, place a check in the right box; if it needs citing, place a check in the left.

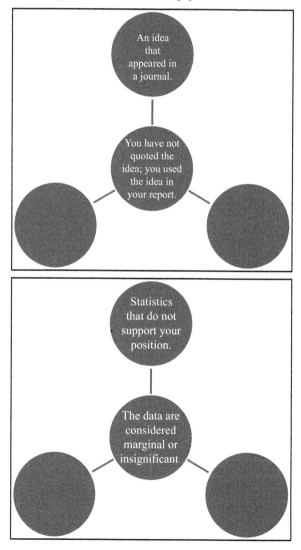

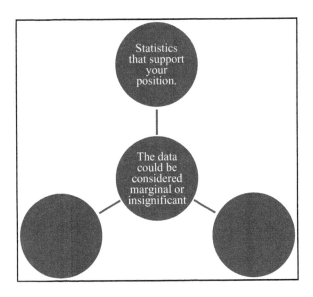

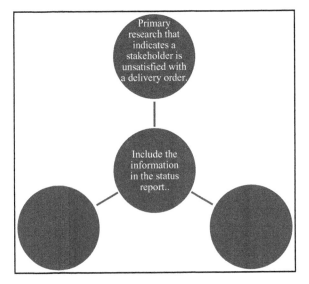

2.2 Finding Reliable Sources

Your job is to find one reliable source for one of the following topics. Be prepared to present your topic to the class in a two- to three-minute presentation.

- Edward R. Murrow
- Joseph McCarthy
- Television news telecasts in the 1950s, specifically CBS news

- Senator Joseph McCarthy
- The House Un-American Activities Committee
- Popular music in the United States in the 1950s that faced censorship
- Types of advertising in the 1950s
- Fred Friendly and/or Joe Wershba

Determine a reliable source from which you found the information. From that point, determine how the information is relevant to present day. You can write a comparison and contrast for this section. This information must not come from other sources; base the information on your prior knowledge, historical facts, and allusions.

2.3 Identifying Follow-Up Questions for Primary Research

Listen to the broadcast of *Digital Music Sampling: Creativity or Criminality?* From NPR. Compose ten open follow-up questions you would ask to expand the interview.

http://www.npr.org/2011/01/28/133306353/ Digital-Music-Sampling-Creativity-Or-Criminality

2.4 Synthesizing Sources through Critical Analysis

Eli's art history professor has assigned a two-page single-spaced report on the influence of art in the nations of Africa. He found an article entitled "African Art and Persuasion: The Rhetoric of the Bera Among the Dargaaba of Ghana," published in the *Journal of Dagaare Studies*. Locate the article, which appears on the doag.org website. Pay close attention to the third section of the article.

Eli's Perception/Text of the Original Source

Based on Eli's synthesizing of the original text, here is what he wants to use in his paper.

Even the Degaara language is considered art. Within this art form, moral lessons are disseminated. "For example, the Dagaaba of Ghana use the word, *viel or viele*, to mean both beautiful and good. When Dagaaba say, *o viela or o vieleng*, they mean that something is beautiful or "it is good." When *o viela or o vieleng* is used to speak about art, the saying indicates that beauty and moral content combine to describe African aesthetics." (Naaeke 23) Several art historians agree that one factor of African art is to convey moral standards. Some African art is made to be ugly just to convey the emotion of fear. Such artist style is used to represent the *bera*. (Naaeke 23)

Works Cited

Naaeke, Anthony. "African Art and Persuasion: The Rhetoric of the Bera Among the Dagaaba of Ghana." *Journal of Dagaare Studies* Vol. 6 (2006): 21–28. Web. DOAJ. 25 May 2012.

When Eli's professor checks his sources, what are the areas in which she will voice her concern? To prevent Eli from getting an F on the paper, identify the errors that you noticed. Offer him suggestions for writing with academic honesty.

First,

> Comment on Eli's writing style.

Second,

> Identify at least three sins of commission and/or omission that Eli has committed.

Third,

Write an academically acceptable version of the paragraph. How can Eli incorporate his writing into the text so that 75% of the text is his? How would you avoid Eli's plagiarism trap?

Fourth,

Examine the References page for "African Art and Persuasion: The Rhetoric of the Bera Among the Dagaaba of Ghana." Identify and comment on any sources that may not pass the reliability test.

Five,

Write a two-page report on African art. Find two reliable sources on the subject that you can incorporate. To narrow your search, locate key words in the article, "African Art and Persuasion: The Rhetoric of the Bera Among the Dagaaba of Ghana." The article appears below in its entirety from the public domain site, DOAJ. Note: Public domain sites allow users to use visuals and text without charge. However, you must cite the source.

2.5 Working in Collaboration

Find a scholarly article on a topic of your choice. The article should not be any longer than four pages, from abstract to conclusion. Read the article and write any comments you may have as you read. Partner with a classmate. Explain the article to your classmate. At this point, do not refer to the article. Your classmate must take notes as you explain the article. Together, write a one-page summary draft of the article without referring to the article.

Compare your summary with the original article. Did you capture the point of the article? Was the original meaning of the article lost? Are there questions that your summary needs to answer?

2.6 Learning about the Subject of an Article

Critical reading involves analyzing and defining unfamiliar terms. Here is the complete article, *Moral and Instrumental Norms in Food Risk Communication*. Circle the words you do not know. Find the definition of the words (be sure to cite the source of the definitions). As you read the article, think about other related subjects; list them. Use the references, abstract, and key words to help you. Next, compose ten research questions to help you understand the article so that you can use it to your professor.

Moral and Instrumental Norms in Food Risk Communication

Peter G. Modin Sven Ove Hansson

Introduction

Moral philosophy is dominated by attempts to specify a consistent, overarching general principle on which all moral judgments can be based. Utilitarianism, deontology, rights-based ethics and virtue ethics all share this approach, although their choices of an overarching principle are different. In contrast, applied ethics tends to be pluralistic and

Springer Science & Business Media. *Journal of Business Ethics*, Vol. 101, No. 2, 2011, pp. 313-324. Peter G. Modin and Sven Ove Hansson. Reprinted with kind permission from Springer Science and Business Media.

operates with a set of rules that is usually not free from conflict. Hence, principles of professional conduct are commonly expressed in ethical codes that are essentially lists of ethical principles for professional activities, and the ethics of organizations is expressed in similarly structured ethical policies (Hansson, 2009). In medical ethics, a dominant approach is the so-called principlism[1] according to which all ethical judgments in medicine should be based on the four principles, viz. autonomy, non-maleficence, beneficence, and justice (O'Neill, 2001). These have been called "intermediate" or "mid-level" principles since they are conceived as intermediate in terms of generality between fundamental moral theories such as utilitarianism on the one hand, and concrete moral advice in specific situations on the other hand. It has been argued that these intermediate principles have the advantage of being justifiable from different moral theories, so that adherents of different such theories can in practice agree on these principles and on the moral judgments that are based on them (Beau champ and Childress, 2001, p. 12).

A major problem with intermediate principles is that to cover the intended subject-area, several such principles are required, and since they are not based on consistent application of some overarching general principle, conflicts between them tend in practice to be unavoidable. It is a common criticism of codes of professional ethics that they contain principles that support contradictory recommendations in controversial cases. As one of many examples, ethical codes for engineers typically urge engineers to be loyal to their employers and also to protect the safety of the public. It is not difficult to find situations in which these two recommendations cannot both be fully satisfied. Similar examples can be found in other such moral codes. Since the four principles have not been derived from a common and unified, consistent base, it is no surprise that they do not provide us with a conflict-free basis for ethical judgments. It is, for instance, not difficult to find conflicts between respect for a patient's autonomy and pursuance of beneficence toward her (Kuczewski, 1998; Takala, 2001).

In spite of this deficiency, the use of some sort of intermediate principles in applied ethics seems difficult to avoid, for the simple reason that fundamental moral theories do not provide us with sufficiently precise advice to handle the problems with which applied ethics is concerned. Scholars with a long experience of serving on ethical committees have observed that differences in opinion on practical issues in bioethics or research ethics have little or no correlation with the discussants' theoretical standpoint in ethics (Heyd, 1996; Kymlicka, 1993; Toulmin, 1981). Philosophers disagree on whether utilitarianism, deontology, virtue ethics, or some other moral theory provides the adequate basis for bioethics. They also disagree on various bioethical issues such as euthanasia, medical paternalism, etc. However, there does not seem to be any correlation between their alignments in these two types of dispute. Hence, utilitarians divide themselves between the various standpoints on euthanasia, and so do virtue ethicists. (An exception must be made for religious ethics. Contrary to secular standpoints, philosophical standpoints based on religions tend to determine the views of their adherents in applied issues such as euthanasia and abortion.)

Hence, fundamental ethical theories seem to be of limited help in dealing with practical ethical issues. Intermediate principles tend to have only loose connections with the fundamental theories. Furthermore, practically relevant systems of intermediate principles seem to lack in coherence and to yield contradictory advice in the difficult cases when we most need moral advice. All this gives us reason to carefully investigate the nature and the status of these intermediate principles.

In this article, we will focus on an issue concerning the application of intermediate principles to practical problems that we discovered in our studies of food risk communication. The general moral recommendations for this area that are found in the literature are intermediate moral principles in the sense referred to above. However, they do not seem to be purely moral principles, since the justifications for them that we found in the literature turned out to be a mixture between moral and instrumental justifications – and often a rather complex mixture in which the two types of justifications are difficult to separate from each other. In order to investigate this phenomenon more in detail, we have condensed the moral advice found in this literature into seven practical principles ("The seven practical principles" section). For each of these, we have investigated how they are justified or justifiable, morally and instrumentally ("Justifications of the seven principles" section). Finally, we discuss the implications of our findings, both for moral philosophy and for practical food risk communication ("Conclusions" section).

The seven practical principles

The academic literature on food risk communication is to a large extent normative. Researchers do not only describe and analyze the communication activities of companies and authorities. More often than not, they also turn normative and comment on what was right and – in particular – on what went wrong in these activities. Case studies are used as sources of lessons on how risk communication can be improved in the future. However, clear-cut recommendations in the form of explicit ethical principles are seldom found in this literature. Instead, recommendations are usually implicit; instead of saying that risk communication should be honest, other authors claim that a risk communication has gone wrong because it was dishonest. In order to discuss the justificatory status of these largely implicit recommendations, we have reconstructed the major (implicit) ethical recommendations that we have found in this literature in the form of seven explicit practical principles:

1. *Be honest and open*: Recommendations to be honest and open are very common in the literature on food risk communication as well as that on risk and crisis communication in general. Such recommendations are often grounded in the need to build credibility and trust (e.g., Frewer, 2003; Phillips Report, 2000; Poortinga and Pidgeon, 2003; Seeger, 2006). According to Frewer et al. (1996), "[t]he most important determinant of gain or loss of trust in a source is whether the source is subsequently proven right or wrong."

2. *Disclose incentives and conflicts of interest*: The injunction to disclose incentives and conflicts of interest is supported, for instance, by Frewer et al. (1996), who assert that particularly in the case of gaining trust, "an important determinant of trust is that the source is subsequently demonstrated to be unbiased." In a review of literature on trust by Renn and Levine (1991), one of the five core components identified was referred to as *objectivity*, the absence of bias. Van Kleef et al. (2007) repeatedly stress the importance of providing unbiased information and not appearing to promote vested interests.

3. *Take all available relevant knowledge into consideration*: Taking all available relevant knowledge into consideration should not be interpreted as implying that every bit of information has to be communicated. Instead it means that one should carefully consider all the available science when deciding what to communicate. The risk communication literature abounds in (divergent) recommendations concerning how much to communicate (as well as how and when to do so, etc.), but most experts agree that the success of risk communication is positively related to the solidity of the foundation upon which the message is based. Frewer et al. (1996) refer to a factor they call

"competence" – the expertise held by the communicator – and assert its importance in determining trust. Based on empirical data, Sjöberg (2006, 2008) concluded that "epistemic trust" – trust in the science on which a risk assessment is based – strongly influences people's reactions to risk communication.

4. *When possible, quantify risks*: One of the most common complaints about risk reporting in the media is that probabilities are left out or not given a sufficiently prominent role (Cray, 2006). This can make it impossible for the recipients of this information to prioritize properly between risks. Providing appropriate quantifications can be seen as part of what is required to make information about a risk comprehensible to its recipients.

5. *Describe and explain uncertainties*: In addition to insuring pertinent facts about the risk itself are understood by the audience, researchers have in recent years pointed out that it can also be beneficial in several ways to communicate information about the scientific uncertainties associated with risk assessments (Frewer, 1999; Kuhn, 2000; Löfstedt, 2006; van Asselt and Vos, 2008).

6. *Take all the public's concerns into account*: An important and often neglected aspect in risk communication is the effects of the public's concerns on their response to risk communication. The public's concerns relate both to those aspects the risk itself the public considers particularly important and other aspects more or less closely related to the risk, for example, animal welfare, the environmental impact of food production, and social or ethical concerns about measures taken to reduce a risk. Recent empirical work supports the conclusion that incorporating the public's point of view into risk management practices is of great importance (Van Kleef et al., 2007). Because people are commonly more closely related to food risks than other risks, as will be developed below, this is particularly important for food risk communication.

7. *Take the rights of individuals and groups seriously*: Our final principle, to pay particular attention to rights, is grounded in the tendency among risk analysts and communicators to focus on whole populations rather than individuals and groups (Hansson, 2007). Most risks do not affect everyone to the same degree (e.g., Frewer, 2004, who refers to this as "risk variability"), which has important implications for risk communication. This, as well as detailed justification of all the principles proposed, is further elaborated in "Justifications of the seven principles" section.

Some of these principles may be partly overlapping. However, they represent what has in the literature usually been treated as different issues or at least as different approaches to the issues at hand. For our present purposes, there was no need to merge these moral injunctions into rules which are broader or more comprehensive than the ones usually referred to in practical discussions of food risk communication. The ethical principles that have been proposed in practice have about this level of generality, presumably because that is the type of principles that is the easiest to use in practice.

The seven principles are all rather general in their formulation, and most if not all of them have been referred to in discussions of communication of other risks than food risks. However, we will focus on the specific subject area of food risks. For several reasons, food risks are special from a communicative point of view: Everyone is concerned by them in her own daily life. We are all dependent on decisions that companies and authorities make on food risks, but at the same time we are also decision makers who choose our own diets. The sheer impossibility of not eating forces us to regularly make food choices, and information about food risks is thus relevant to and has the potential of affecting our decisions on a daily basis. Decisions on food choice are closely linked not only (trivially) to the palatability of the food (e.g., Pliner and Mann, 2004) but also to lifestyles and to cultural, traditional and sometimes religious or even political values which are often important for people's social identity. The fact that food is inserted into our own bodies and those of our children seems to make food risks particularly sensitive and emotionally laden. Healthiness, perceived riskiness, and cultural/traditional/religious values are often at odds, pointing the individual who needs to make a choice concerning what to eat in different directions. All of this combines to make the communication of food risks particularly difficult. We should not take for granted that the relation between moral and instrumental justification is necessarily the same for food risks as in other areas of risk communication.

Justifications of the seven principles

On the face of it, the distinction between a moral and an instrumental justification is simple and straightforward. A typical moral justification of honesty would consist in showing that dishonesty is morally wrong, e.g., because it violates some more fundamental moral principles. A typical instrumental justification would be one that shows that dishonesty makes it more difficult to achieve non-moral goals, e.g., because dishonesty will sooner or later be discovered and then make the public suspicious of the organization.

A more careful investigation of the distinction between moral and instrumental justification will show that it is in fact quite problematic since the two concepts represent overlapping categories rather than the two endpoints of one and the same distinction. A justification could for instance refer to a moral principle that is not a final end but a means for some other, final moral end. Such a justification would be both moral and instrumental. Furthermore, a justification could be neither moral nor instrumental, namely if it refers to some final end that is not of a moral kind. However, in studying the literature on food risk communication we have not found any justifications that cause problems for the simplified dichotomy in any of these two ways. The distinction that we are primarily interested in is that between justification in moral and non-moral terms.

The justifications of the latter type which we have found to be relevant in this area are those that refer to how adherence to an ethical principle creates instrumental value in terms of the self-interest of the communicating organization. We will refer to this as a moral/instrumental dichotomy since this terminology has the advantage of being generally known and easily understood.

We will focus on the two types of communicating organizations whose activities have been at focus in the academic literature: companies producing and selling foodstuff, and government agencies with a responsibility for food safety. Hence our conclusions do not necessarily apply to other communicators such as NGOs active in the area of food risks.

As we have already emphasized, although the literature on food risk communication is replete with normative statements and recommendations, ethical principles are often implicit (for instance in criticism of purportedly unethical behavior) and argumentation for them is often fragmentary or absent. Therefore, we will not restrict our discussion of justifications to previously published justifications but will also discuss the justifiability of the above-mentioned seven principles in moral and instrumental terms.

Be honest and open

There is no lack of argumentation in the ethical literature for the position that dishonesty is morally wrong. The topic has been discussed by innumerable scholars throughout the centuries. Two prominent examples are St. Thomas Aquinas and Immanuel Kant, who both condemn lying strongly. The former discusses lying [partly in response to an earlier treatise on the subject by St. Augustine (*De Mendacio*)] in *Summa Theologica* (Aquinas, 1271/1981). He essentially argues that lying, defined as asserting a falsehood with the intention to deceive, is always wrong (Finnis, 2008; Westberg, 2002, p. 95). Aquinas' argument appears to be based on the intentional dissonance between the liar's self presented through her assertion of something she believes to be false, and her real self. Finnis (2008) writes: "Whenever one asserts, one affirms as true two propositions: explicitly the proposition one articulates as true despite one's belief that it is not, and implicitly the proposition that one believes what one is assertively articulating."

Kant's argument against lying resembles Aquinas' in that it, too, is based on self-contradiction. In brief, Kant (1785/1998) argues that it is forbidden to perform an action if that action made into universal law contradicts itself. Thus, lying to get what one wants is forbidden, since the universal law 'everyone should lie to get what they want' is irrational and self-contradictory: in a world where everyone lies, lying to get what you want would serve no purpose, because everyone would expect you to lie and no-one would accept a promise.[2] This is a far-reaching argument against lying, applicable to risk communicators and everyone else alike.

In the utilitarian tradition, lying is not universally prohibited, but has to be judged according to the moral value of its consequences. However, utilitarians have been eager to show that untruthfulness has so bad consequences that it is very seldom justified. Hence, in his *Utilitarianism*, Mill recognizes that "it would often be expedient, for the purpose of ... attaining some object immediately useful to ourselves or others, to tell a lie," but he maintains that untruthfulness has the long-term negative consequences of weakening the trustworthiness of human assertion, which is "the principal support of all present social well-being" and the lack of which keeps back "civilization, virtue, everything on which human happiness on the largest scale depends" (Mill, 1863/1969, p. 223). When these long-term consequences are taken into account, lying will in most cases have predominantly negative consequences, and is therefore not allowed from a utilitarian point of view. In a letter to Henry Sidgwick, Mill said that there ought to be "some, however few, exceptions" to what he called "the obligation of veracity" or "the general duty of truth" (Mill, 1991, p. 185).

Mill's terminology in this letter is interesting, since a duty to (tell the) truth to clearly goes beyond the mere avoidance of lying. In modern discussions of food risk communication, such a wide duty of truthfulness seems to be implicated. Critics of deceitful or secretive behavior by agencies and companies tend to be critical not only against untruthful statements but also against the withholding of information from people who want it. Goldman (1991) introduced the term *epistemic paternalism* to refer to the withholding of information from people for their alleged own good. Grill and Hansson (2005) discuss this in a context of threats to public health that includes food risks. They argue that there are strong consequentialist arguments against the application of epistemic paternalism in public health issues. Although withholding information may be the best way to achieve a short-term, well-defined objective, it leads to an erosion of trust that has larger negative consequences in the long run.

In the food risk communication literature, the same argument structure is often applied to show that truthfulness is instrumentally best in the long run. Although lying or withholding information can be expedient in the short run, in the long run this has negative effects on trust. Lack of trust will severely impede the agent's future efforts in risk communication (Frewer et al., 1996; Finucane and Holup, 2005; Löfstedt, 2005, 2006; Poortinga and Pidgeon, 2003, 2004). Meijboom et al. (2006) and van Dijk et al. (2008) specifically discuss and assert the importance of trust and openness in the food sector.

Traditionally, the focus in this discussion has been on trust in general, e.g., 'social' trust in institutions and experts. However, some empirical work indicates that epistemic trust – trust in the science on which a risk assessment or risky technology is based – explains this effect better than trust in general (Sjöberg, 2006, 2008; Sjöberg and Wester-Herber, 2008). Several authors have pointed out that honesty and openness promote both social and epistemic trust (Frewer et al., 2003; Seeger, 2006; Van Kleef et al., 2007).

In summary, the first practical principle has credible justifications both in moral and in instrumental terms. Furthermore, the argument structure tends to be similar for the two types of arguments.

Disclose incentives and conflicts of interest

Food risk issues are often scientifically controversial. Assessments of risk are largely based on indirect evidence such as animal data. The reason for this is that harmful effects can often be discovered in this way before effects have been demonstrated in humans. Since food risk assessments are largely based on such indirect evidence, they depend on professional judgment, which may differ between experts. Studies from other areas show that the judgments of experts may be significantly influenced by conflicts of interest. Based on interviews with 136 scientists working for industry, academia and government, Lynn (1986) found significant differences between scientists with different affiliations in their attitudes toward questions such as the existence of thresholds and the value of animal models in identifying human risk. Barnes and Bero (1998) studied 106 review articles on the health effects of passive smoking and found a significant correlation between the conclusion of a review and its author's affiliation; reviews concluding that passive smoking does not harm human health were predominantly written by authors affiliated with the tobacco industry.

The injunction that experts and others who communicate food risks should disclose their affiliations and other connections which may amount to a conflict of interest can be supported by the same type of ethical arguments as those used for our first principle. Assuming that truthfulness to the public is morally required, this truthfulness would have to include any information that may legitimately influence their appraisal of the experts' statements. It is no coincidence that in biomedical publication, publication of conflict of interest statements is considered to be an ethical issue (ICMJE, 2008).

From an instrumental point of view, conflicts of interest have turned out to be very difficult to conceal in the long run. Non-disclosure can delay public knowledge of conflicts of interest, but cannot be expected to exclude it indefinitely. The effects of the ultimate disclosure can be devastating. An organization or person who has misrepresented their loyalties will find it very difficult to regain the public's trust, once the deception has been disclosed (Frewer et al., 1996). As was noted by Frewer (2004), "[…] if a distrusted source provides information that appears to promote its own vested interest, the information will influence people's attitudes in the opposite direction to that being promoted in the first place" (cf. Sjöberg and Wester-Herber, 2008; Van Kleef et al., 2007). In summary, there are strong justifications of both an ethical and an instrumental nature for the disclosure of incentives and conflicts of interest.

Take all available, relevant knowledge into consideration

Food risk issues are often scientifically complex. The data may point in different directions, some studies indicating a higher degree of risks than others. One should therefore expect risk communication to be based on careful assessments of all the available literature. However, studies of risk assessments show that they are often surprisingly incomplete, taking into account some but not all of the available information that could have influenced the risk assessment (Rudén, 2004). Sometimes the exclusion of relevant information may be driven by bias, and on other occasions, it is due to lack of resources or competence. Our third practical principle requires that in the preparation of messages to be communicated to the public, the available knowledge should be taken into consideration as completely as possible. This recommendation should not be confused with a requirement to include all the available knowledge in the message. Recipients of communication about food risks are best served by information aimed specifically at them as a target group, composed with relevant properties of that group borne in mind.[3] For many target groups, relatively brief and non-technical summaries of the scientific information are appropriate. However, in the preparation of such messages the whole range of available evidence has to be carefully scrutinized.

A fairly straight-forward justification of this standpoint in ethical terms can be based on the truthfulness condition discussed in "Be honest and open" section. Similarly, an instrumental justification can be based on the same type of argumentation that was introduced in that section. An agency or company that bases its communications and recommendations on only part of the available knowledge takes a considerable risk in doing so. If the excluded information gives reason to change the public message, then the organization loses much of its credibility when the excluded information becomes available to the public. This seems to have happened to British authorities during the BSE crisis (Phillips Report, 2000; van Zwanenberg and Millstone, 2002). Information that indicated that it was not completely safe to eat British meat was not included in information from authorities to the public, and when the public received that information the credibility of the authorities was severely damaged (Leiss et al., 2004).

In summary, the injunction to take all the available knowledge into account can easily be justified with both moral and instrumental arguments.

When possible, quantify risks

A common complaint in the risk analysis literature is that the public allegedly treats small and large risks alike. This applies not least in the literature on food risks. It has repeatedly been pointed out for instance that small pesticide residues are given a too high priority in public debates as compared to the more general issue of a balanced diet at an appropriate caloric level (Abelson, 1995). Although probabilistic risk assessment does not necessarily tell us all we need to know about a risk, the probability that a danger will materialize is certainly one of the factors which should be taken into account in the assessment of that danger. Equally obviously, a decision-maker needs to be informed of the nature of the negative effect to which a risk refers. Important aspects of its nature are often best expressed in quantitative terms, e.g., the number of people expected to be killed in a fatal accident or the economic costs in a case of damage to property.

In the case of food risk communication, relative risks are often used in communications to the public. Newspaper reports often tell us that a particular characteristic of the diet leads to a "doubled risk" of some disease. However, relative risks are difficult to interpret unless one knows the baseline frequency. A relative risk of 2.0 can be negligible for a rare disease but a major concern if the disease is common. Absolute risk estimates are usually more informative for the individual. A person who wants to decrease the total risk of having her health impaired by bad food should give priority to avoiding the high absolute risks, rather than the high relative risks. In the BBC guidelines for journalistic reporting of risks, quantitative measures of risk have an important role (Löfstedt, 2006). Research by Krystallis et al. (2007) has also demonstrated that members of the public sometimes perceive that they reach a state of "information overload." This highlights the importance of providing information of good quality, i.e., information quantified and worded in accordance with the needs of the target group (Van Kleef et al., 2007).

An ethical justification of this principle can be derived from the truthfulness criterion to which we have already appealed repeatedly. For an instrumental justification, it is useful in this case to distinguish between public authorities and companies. A public authority expectedly has a mandate to give higher priority to a danger with a high probability than to an otherwise similar danger with a low probability. Therefore, in order to fulfil its task, the authority has to encourage other actors to make similar priorities. When it comes to a company producing a potentially harmful product, a distinction should be made between the cases when the public tends to overestimate respectively underestimate the relevant properties (e.g., the probability and severity of harm) of the risk. In the former case, it is obviously in the company's business interest to promote knowledge of these properties. In the second case, the instrumental necessity of truthfulness to obtain trust that we have repeatedly referred to above will give the company reason to promote a correct understanding of the probabilities and effects involved. Otherwise, it runs the risk of being accused of not providing the public with the information it needs to make well-informed food choices. If such accusations can be substantiated, they may have devastating effects from a purely business-related point of view.

Hence, this principle has both and ethical and instrumental justifications.

Describe and explain uncertainties

The term "uncertainty" is used in decision analysis to denote such lack of knowledge which cannot be described adequately with an exact probability value. In a classic textbook in decision theory, uncertainty was defined as a decision situation where at least one option "has as its consequence a set of possible specific outcomes, but where the probabilities of these outcomes are completely unknown or are not even meaningful" (Luce and Raiffa, 1957, p. 13). In later work, the term "uncertainty" has also been used to describe situations where probabilities can be assigned but must be seen as approximate or preliminary.

In practice, the scientific documentation on food risks always contains uncertainties which make it impossible to set exact probabilities with certainty. Uncertainty about food risk may depend on lack of data, on confounding factors and insufficient sensitivity in the available studies, on methodological limits to the sensitivity of any studies that can be performed (Hansson, 1999), on problems in cross-species extrapolation, etc. Even if these uncertainties cannot be expressed in probabilistic terms, it is possible and meaningful to describe the uncertainties and to inform those who receive information about risks about how uncertain various statements about the harmfulness or harmlessness of different exposures are. Such information is important for decision-makers, since their decisions may depend on it. Suppose for instance that there is a choice between two food preservatives, A and B. The estimated risk of negative health effects is equally low for both of them, but the scientific documentation about A is much better than that about B, and consequently the uncertainty about A's health effects is smaller than that about B's health effects. A manufacturer choosing between A and B should be informed about this, and would probably prefer the less uncertain alternative (A). Similarly, a member of the public who chooses between otherwise similar products containing A respectively B would expectedly want to know the difference in terms of uncertainty, and would probably use the information in the corresponding way, i.e., avoid the more uncertain option.[4] It was previously thought that the general public has a hard time understanding uncertainties; however, recent research has shown that this is not always so, and than risk communication audience want that type of information (Frewer et al., 2002).

From a moral point of view, respect of other decision-makers' autonomy requires that they are provided with the information that would influence their decisions. Since information about uncertainty tends to influence the public's decisions, they should have access to such information. From an instrumental point of view, risk communicators loose the audience's trust if they do not report uncertainties (Jensen and Sandøe, 2002). One of the major lessons from the BSE case is that a public authority that describes scientific information as more certain than it is loses its credibility if the public later learns that it downplayed the uncertainties (Miles and Frewer, 2003; Millstone et al., 2006; Phillips Report, 2000).

Take all the public's concerns into account

In standard risk analysis, risk is perceived as constituted of two components, the probability and the severity of harm. Hence, the International Organization for Standardization (2002) defines risk as "the combination of the probability of an event and its consequences." One of the major reasons why the public is often dissatisfied with the outcome of professional risk analysis is that risk analysts leave out other factors such as the distribution of risks, whether risk-taking was voluntary, the relation between risk-imposers and risk-exposed, etc. (Hermansson and Hansson, 2007). It has been known for some time that these factors are relevant and important to risk perception and acceptance (Slovic, 1987, 1993), and from a moral point of view, it would be difficult to claim that they are irrelevant.

The relevance of factors in addition to probability and severity seems to be even larger for food risks than for most other risks. Food risks are special in that everyone ingests food and also makes his or her own choices between different food items (Löfstedt, 2006). These choices are influenced by a wide range of issues not directly related to health risks:

Social, religious and cultural traditions have a large impact on our food choices. New lifestyles often involve changes in food habits, as evidenced by the adoption of vegetarianism in some social sectors. Environmental concerns, animal welfare, worldview-related resistance to GMOs, solidarity with exploited farm workers in developing countries, and a negative view of certain (typically multinational) food companies are other factors that influence some consumers' choice of food. Miles and Frewer (2001) note that psychological concerns about food risks should be subject to particular investigation since they are likely to be unique to the food domain.

From a moral point of view it would be next to absurd to claim that food-related decisions should be based only on health aspects. Several of the additional concerns just mentioned have obvious moral relevance, and should be treated accordingly. Therefore, authorities and companies that communicate with the public should take the public's concerns seriously, and not dismiss them as irrelevant without studying them carefully. Furthermore, respect for consumers' autonomy as decision-makers is often a strong reason for providing them with the information they want when making their choices of food items, even if the criteria the choices are based on have no scientific foundation. Some consumers may want to know if the food they eat is halal, kosher, made of dog or horse meat, genetically modified, grown without use of pesticides, etc. Denying them access to such information with the motivation that the information is irrelevant for assessing the healthiness of the food would amount to denying them the right to make their own decisions on what type of food they want to eat.

From an instrumental point of view, dismissing the public's concerns tends to result in a decline in public confidence (Van Kleef et al., 2007). Again, we can use the BSE case as an example. One of the major (moral) concerns of the public, "making cows into cannibals" by feeding them bone meal, was largely ignored by public authorities during the crisis. Previous research has demonstrated that if societal values are not integrated in the risk analysis, subsequent risk management activities may appear to promote particular vested interests (Van Kleef et al., 2007; cf. "Disclose incentives and conflicts of interest" section above), and the public looses trust in risk assessment and management (Frewer et al., 2005).

It should be noted that this need to take the public's concerns and values into account implies that good risk communication necessarily must involve communicating *with* the public rather than just sending messages *to* the public. Input from the public, stakeholder involvement and public engagement in the risk management process can increase transparency and consumer trust, provided that the way these inputs are used is also communicated back to the public (Jensen, 2006; Rowe and Frewer, 2005).

Take the rights of individuals and groups seriously

In professional risk analysis, risks are usually treated on an aggregated level (Hansson, 2004). This means that risks (and corresponding benefits) are added up, and judged according to the sum, irrespective of how that sum is distributed. The use of this approach for analytic purposes tends to encourage the view that the justification of risk-taking can follow the same structure, i.e., refer only to the total amount of risk-taking and disregard how it is distributed. In actual social contexts, this does not work. Actual social morality does not operate on the aggregated level but on the individual level. People have *rights* not to be unfairly treated or exposed to unreasonable risk by others. The language of rights is indeed often used by persons who consider themselves to be subject to unjustified or illegitimate risk-exposure: They claim that they have a right to be informed about unhealthy components in food, that the local factory has no right to poison the air they breathe, etc.

From a moral point of view, it is evident that rights are involved in situations of risk. We all have rights not to be injured by others, and we have corresponding duties not to injure them. We have no right to kill other persons; neither do we have a right to expose them to great danger of death. Selling food that is sure to kill the consumers is obviously immoral (and legally prohibited); the same applies to food that has a large probability of killing the person who eats it. The difficult question is where to draw the limit; requiring zero probability would be infeasible. We will not try to solve this issue here [but see Hansson (2003) for a discussion of some relevant aspects]. For our present purposes, the essential conclusion is that rights (of groups and individuals) are an inescapable component of the moral discourse on food risks. This is sufficient for the moral justification of our seventh principle. Its instrumental justification is obvious: Treating risks on the aggregate level, without considering the rights of the people who may be exposed to the risks seems to be an infallible way of turning these people against you. This is a lesson that many organizations have learnt the hard way, and to avoid making this mistake, it is necessary for risk communicators to make sure individuals and groups get access to the information that is relevant to their specific needs (Scherer and Juanillo, 1992).

Conclusions

All the seven principles for food risk communication that we have identi-fied as central in the literature turn out to be easily justifiable not only from a moral but also from an instrumental point of view. (Our usage of these terms was clarified in "Introduction" section.) The generality of this result need not be overemphasized. There may be some other reasonable moral injunctions for food risk communication that we have failed to identify, and for which no credible instrumental justification can be given. However, in spite of extensive search, we have not been able to find any such principle. Neither have we been able to find a clear example of a particular action in food risk communication that some authority or company is morally required to perform but does not have an instrumental justification to perform. Although the harmony may not be perfect, there seems to be a high degree of harmony between ethical and instrumental justifications in this area.

Of course, this harmony does not extend to the ethics of organiza-tional behavior in general. We do not wish to claim that reasonable moral requirements on companies or other organizations are always in compli-ance with enlightened self-interest. In all probability, the profit-making capacity of a weapons industry is inversely related to the ethical stan-dards it applies in its choice of customers.

Why then do we find this harmony between ethical and instrumental justifications in the area of food risk communications? As far as we can see, it depends on a simple fact about the ethical requirements in this case: *The ethical requirements all consist in serving the interests of those who consume the product.* The ethical requirements on food risk communication, at least as discussed in media and in the academic literature, are all of that nature. For ethical requirements that satisfy this criterion, it can be expected that "consciousness-raising" activities, making companies aware of what they can gain from satisfying the requirements, should be efficient. The same type of measures should expectedly also have some effects for other requirements towards which costumers in general tend to be sympathetic. Examples for the food industry include requirements to reduce its negative environmental impact and to improve animal welfare. As we have already mentioned, there are also ethical requirements on companies that are not supported by enlightened self-interest. In an implementation-oriented eth-ical discourse, it is useful to differentiate between these different catego-ries, since they may give rise to quite different implementation strategies.

Notes

1 The principles have been defended by Tom Beauchamp and James Childress since the 1970s (Beauchamp, 1994; Beauchamp and Childress, 2001); the term "principlism" was coined by their critics K. Danner Clouser and Bernard Gert in their article *A Critique of Principalism* (1990).

2 For further details on Kant's moral philosophy, see, e.g., Kant's discussion of the example of lying as constituting a perfect duty to others in *On a supposed right to lie because of philanthropic concerns*, published as a supplement to the *Groundwork for the Metaphysics of Morals*, and Johnson (2010). For further details on Aquinas' moral philosophy, see Pope (2002).

3 Such properties can be, e.g., prior knowledge, whether that group is more or less at risk than other groups, factors that may increase or decrease risk perception and/or aversion, etc.

4 It should be noted that products rarely differ only in the uncertainty of the product's riskiness. Other properties of products – typically, cost and palatability in the case of food products – also tend to influence the decision concerning which product to buy. It is consequently of great importance that uncertainties are communicated and explained well in order that the uncertainty information be able to exert the appropriate influence (in competition with other pertinent factors) on those making the choices.

References

Abelson, P. H.: 1995, 'Exaggerated Risks of Chemicals', *Journal of Clinical Epidemiology* **48**, 173–178.

Aquinas, St. T.: 1271/1981, *Summa Theologica* (Sheed & Ward, London).

Barnes, D. E. and L. A. Bero: 1998, 'Why Review Articles on the Health Effects of Passive Smoking Reach Different Conclusions', *JAMA* **279**(19), 1566–1570.

Beauchamp, T. L.: 1994, 'Principlism and Its Alleged Competitors', *Kennedy Institute of Ethics Journal* 5(3), 181–198.

Beauchamp, T. L. and J. F. Childress: 2001, *Principles of Biomedical Ethics*, 5th Edition (Oxford University Press, New York).

Cray, D.: 2006, 'How we Confuse Real Risks with Exaggerated Ones', *Time*, Nov. 29.

Finnis, J.: 2008, Aquinas' Moral, Political, and Legal Philosophy', in E. N. Zalta (ed.), *The Stanford Encyclopedia of Philosophy*, fall 2008 edition. http://plato.stanford.edu/archives/fall2008/entries/aquinas-moral-political/.

Finucane, M. L. and J. L. Holup: 2005, 'Psychosocial and Cultural Factors Affecting the Perceived Risk of Genetically Modified Food: An Overview of the Literature', *Social Science and Medicine* **60**, 1603–1612.

Frewer, L. J.: 1999, 'Risk Perception, Social Trust, and Public Participation into Strategic Decision-Making – Implications for Emerging Technologies', *Ambio* **28**, 569–574.

Frewer, L. J.: 2003, Briefing Paper: Consumer Science Implications for the Interface of Risk Assessment and Risk Management. European Workshop on the Interface between Risk Assessment and Risk Management, 2003.

Frewer, L. J.: 2004, 'The Public and Effective Risk Communication', *Toxicology Letters* **149**, 391–397.

Frewer, L. J., C. Howard, D. Hedderley and R. Shepherd: 1996, 'What Determines Trust in Information About Food-Related Risks? Underlying Psychological Constructs', *Risk Analysis* **16**(4), 473–486.

Frewer, L. J., A. Koles, S. van de Kroon and C. Lawere: 2005, 'Consumer Acceptance of Animal Husbandry Systems', *Journal of Agricultural and Environmental Ethics* **18**, 345–367.

Frewer, L. J., S. Miles, M. Brennan, S. Kuznesof, M. Ness and C. Ritson: 2002, 'Public Preferences for Informed Choice Under Conditions of Risk Uncertainty', *Public Understanding of Science* **11**, 363–372.

Frewer, L. J., J. Scholderer and L. Bredahl: 2003, 'Communicating About the Risks and Benefits of Genetically Modified Foods: The Mediating Role of Trust', *Risk Analysis* **23**(6), 1117–1133.

Goldman, A. I.: 1991, 'Epistemic Paternalism', *Journal of Philosophy* **88**, 113–131.

Grill, K. and S. O. Hansson: 2005, 'Epistemic Paternalism in Public Health', *Journal of Medical Ethics* **19**(11).

Hansson, S. O.: 1999, 'The Moral Significance of Indetectable Effects', *Risk* **10**, 101–108.

Hansson, S. O.: 2003, 'Ethical Criteria of Risk Acceptance', *Erkenntnis* **59**, 291–309.

Hansson, S. O.: 2004, 'Weighing Risks and Benefits', *Topoi* **23**, 145–152.

Hansson, S. O.: 2007, 'The Ethics of Communicating Public Health Research', *Harvard Health Policy Review* **8**(2), 158–165.

Hansson, S. O.: 2009, 'Ethics Beyond Application', in T. Takala, P. Heris-sone-Kelly and S. Holm (eds.), *Cutting Through the Surface: Philosophical Approaches to Bioethics* (Rodopi, Amsterdam and New York).

Hermansson, H, and S. O. Hansson: 2007, 'A Three Party Model Tool for Ethi-cal Risk Analysis', *Risk Management* **9**(3), 129–144.

Heyd, D.: 1996, 'Experimenting with Embryos: Can Philosophy Help?', *Bioeth-ics* **10**, 292–309.

ICMJE (208) Uniform Requirements for Manuscripts Submitted to Biomedi-cal Journals: Writing and Editing for Biomedical Publication. October 2008 version. International Committee of Medical Journal Editiors, http://www.icmje.org/icmje.pdf. Accessed May 2009.

International Organization for Standardization: 2002, Risk Management – Vocabulary – Guildelines for Use in Standards, ISO/IEC Guide 73:2002.

Jensen, K. K.: 2006, 'Conflict Over Risks in Food Production: A Challenge for Democracy', *Journal of Agricultural and Environmental Ethics* **19**, 269–283.

Jensen, K. K. and P. Sandoe: 2002, 'Food Safety and Ethics: The Interplay Between Science and Values', *Journal of Agricultural and Environmental Eth-ics* **15**, 245–253.

Johnson, R.: 2010, 'Kant's Moral Philosophy', in E. N. Zalta (ed.), *The Stanford Encyclopedia of Philosophy* (Summer 2010 Edition), http://plato.stanford.edu/archives/sum2010/entries/kant-moral/.

Kant, I.: 1785/1998, *Groundwork of the Metaphysics of Morals* (Cambridge University Press, Cambridge).

Krystallis, A., L. J. Frewer, G. Rowe, J. Houghton, O. Kehagia and T. Perrea: 2007, 'A Perceptual Divide? Consumer and Expert Attitudes to Food Risk Management in Europe', *Health, Risk and Society* **9**(4), 407–424.

Kuczewski, M.: 1998, 'Casuistry and Principlism: The Convergence of Method in Biomedical Ethics', *Theoretical Medicine and Bioethics* **19**, 509–524.

Kuhn, K. M.: 2000, 'Message Format and Audience Values, Interactive Effects of Uncertainty Information and Environmental Attitudes on Perceived Risk', *Journal of Environmental Psychology* **20**, 41–57.

Kymlicka, W.: 1993, 'Moral Philosophy and Public Policy: The Case of the New Reproductive Technologies', *Bioethics* **7**, 1–26.

Leiss, W., D. Powell and A. Whitfield: 2004, 'Med Cows or Crazy Communications?', in W. Leiss and D. Powell (eds.), *Mad Cows and Mother's Milk: The Perils of Poor Risk Communication* (McGill-Queen's University Press, Montreal).

Löfstedt, R. E.: 2005, *Risk Management in Post Trust Societies* (Palgrave Macmillan, Basingstoke).

Löfstedt, R. E.: 2006, 'How can we Make Food Risk Communication Better: Where are we and Where are we Going?', *Journal of Risk Research* 9(8), 869–890.

Luce, R. D. and D. Raiffa: 1957, *Games and Decisions: Introduction and Critical Survey* (Wiley, New York).

Lynn, F. M.: 1986, "The Interplay of Science and Values in Assessing and Regulating Environmental Risks', *Science, Technology, & Human Values* 11(2), 40–50.

Meijboom, F. L. B., T. Visak and F. W. A. Brom: 2006, 'From Trust to Trustworthiness: Why Information is not Enough in the Food Sector', *Journal of Agricultural and Environmental Ethics* 19, 427–442.

Miles, S. and L. J. Frewer: 2001, 'Investigating Specific Concerns About Different Food Hazards', *Food Quality and Preference* 12, 47–61.

Miles, S. and L. J. Frewer: 2003, 'Public Perception of Scientific Uncertainty in Relation to Food Hazards', *Journal of Risk Research* 6(3), 267–283.

Mill, J. S.: 1863/1969, 'Utilitarianism', in J. M. Robson (ed.), *Collected Works of John Stuart Mill. Vol. 10, Essays on Ethics, Religion and Society* (University of Toronto Press, Toronto).

Mill, J. S.: 1991, in M. Filipiuk (ed.), *Collected Works of John Stuart Mill. Vol. 32, Additional Letters of John Stuart Mill* (University of Toronto Press, Toronto).

Millstone, E., P. van Zwanenberg, M. Bauer, C. Dora, E. Dowler, A. Draper, K. Dressel, G. Gasperoni, J. Greeen, M. Koivusalo and E. Ollila: 2006, 'Chapter 10: Improving Communication Strategies and Engaging with Public Concerns', in C. Dora (ed.), *Health and Hazard Public Debate: Lessons for Risk Communication from the BSE/CJD saga* (WHO Europe, Copenhagen).

O'Neill, O.: 2001, 'Practical Principles and Practical Judgment', *Hastings Center Report* 31(4), 15–23.

Phillips Report: 2000, *The BSE Inquiry: The Report. The Inquiry into BSE and CJD in the United Kingdom* (The Stationary Office, London).

Pliner, P. and N. Mann: 2004, 'Influence of social norms and palatability on amount consumed and food choice', *Appetite* **42**, 227–237.

Poortinga, W. and N. F. Pidgeon: 2003, 'Exploring the Dimensionality of Trust in Risk Regulation', *Risk Analysis* **23**(5), 961–972.

Poortinga, W. and N. F. Pidgeon: 2004, "Trust, the Asymmetry Principle, and the Role of Prior Beliefs', *Risk Analysis* **24**(6), 1475–1486.

Pope, S. J. (ed.): 2002, *The Ethics of Aquinas* (Georgetown University Press, Washington, DC).

Renn, O. and D. Levine: 1991, 'Credibility and Trust in Risk Communication', in R. E. Kasperson and P. J. M. Stallen (eds.), *Communicating Risks to the Public* (Kluwer, The Hague).

Rowe, G. and L. J. Frewer: 2005, 'A Typology of Public Engagement Mechanisms', *Sciene, Technology and Human Values* **30**(2), 251–290.

Rudén, C.: 2004, 'Acrylamide and Cancer Risk – Expert Risk Assessments and the Public Debate', *Food and Chemical Taxicology* **42**, 335–349.

Scherer, C. W. and N. K. Juanillo: 1992, Communicating Food Safety: Ethical Issues in Risk Communication. *Agriculture and Human Values* **9** (Spring issue), 17–26.

Seeger, M. W.: 2006, 'Best Practices in Crisis Communication: An Expert Panel Process', *Journal of Applied Communication Research* **34**(3), 232–244.

Sjöberg, L.: 2006, Myths of the Psychometric Paradigm and how they can Misinform Risk Communication. Paper presented at the conference "New Perspectives on Risk Communication: Uncertainty in a Complex Society" Göteborg University, 31 August–2 September, 2006.

Sjöberg, L.: 2008, 'Genetically Modified Food in the Eyes of the Public and Experts', *Risk Management* **10**, 168–193.

Sjöberg, L. and M. Wester–Herber: 2008, 'Too Much Trust in (Social) Trust? The Importance of Epistemic Concerns and Perceived Antagonism', *International Journal of Global Environmental Issues* **30**(1–2), 30–44.

Slovic, P.: 1987, 'Perception of Risk', *Science* **236**, 280–285.

Slovic, P.: 1993, 'Perceived Risk, Trust, and Democracy', *Risk Analysis* **13**(6), 675–682.

Takala, T.: 2001, 'What is Wrong with Global Bioethics? On the Limitations of the Four Principles Approach', *Cambridge Quarterly of Healthcare Ethics* **10**, 72–77.

Toulmin, S.: 1981, 'The Tyranny of Principles – Regaining the Ethics of Discretion', *Hastings Center Report* **11**, 31–38.

van Asselt, M. B. A. and E. Vos: 2008, 'Wrestling with Uncertain Risks: EU Regulation of GMOs and the Uncertainty Paradox', *Journal of Risk Research* **11**(1–2), 281–300.

van Dijk, H., J. Houghton, E. van Kleef, I. van der Lans, G. Rowe and L. Frewer: 2008, 'Consumer Responses to Communication about Food Risk Management', *Appetite* **50**, 340–352.

Van Kleef, E., J. R. Houghton, A. Krystallis, U. Pfenning, G. Rowe, H. Van Dijk, I. A. Van der Lans and L. J. Frewer: 2007, 'Consumer Evaluations of Food Risk Management Quality in Europe', *Risk Analysis* **27**(6), 1565–1580.

van Zwanenberg, P. and E. Millstone: 2002, *BSE: Risk and Regulation* (UK National Consumer Council, London).

Westberg, D.: 2002, 'Good and Evil in Human Acts', in S. J. Pope (ed.), *The Ethics of Aquinas* (Georgetown University Press, Washington, DC).

KTH (Royal Institute of Technology),
Stockholm, Sweden
E-mail: modin@kth.se;
soh@kth.se

2.7 Analyzing a Visual for Content and Design

A visual that contains various visual stimuli can be difficult to read and interpret. Find a visual that contains statistical data on the popularity of social media. Are the statistics easily verifiable? If not, where must you look to confirm the information? Is the website reliable? Why or why not? Are there sins of commission or omission? What additional information would you need to know for the visual to stand on its own?

2.8 Checklists and Response Cards

Time management is essential in research writing (Tip One). Complete the following checklists and response cards for each source. Use the information to determine whether you can compose a document in which your writing will shine through.

Note: Make copies as necessary. Three copies are provided for you.

What is the originator's thesis or point of view?	What is the author saying? If you cannot determine the answer to this question, what words do you need to define to help you understand?	What information/topics can you add to the text to incorporate into your writing?

Use: Quote, Paraphrase, Summary	Information	Source Information (date, author/ editor, type of source, publisher, name of source, URL, page number)	Reason for use— What type of support does it provide?

What is the originator's thesis or point of view?	What is the author saying? If you cannot determine the answer to this question, what words do you need to define to help you understand?	What information/topics can you add to the text to incorporate into your writing?

Use: Quote, Paraphrase, Summary	Information	Source Information (date, author/ editor, type of source, publisher, name of source, URL, page number)	Reason for use— What type of support does it provide?

What is the originator's thesis or point of view?	What is the author saying? If you cannot determine the answer to this question, what words do you need to define to help you understand?	What information/topics can you add to the text to incorporate into your writing?

Use: Quote, Paraphrase, Summary	Information	Source Information (date, author/ editor, type of source, publisher, name of source, URL, page number)	Reason for use—What type of support does it provide?

CHAPTER

3

Document and Cite Correctly

Numerous style guides and documentation styles are available for writers to ensure proper source acknowledgement This chapter provides examples of APA and MLA citation and documentation format to ensure that you understand how to acknowledge reliable sources in your writing by:

- Citing and documenting in APA and MLA style
- Analyzing a student example to recognize how to strengthen your writing
- Writing an annotated bibliography as a means to test the validity of a source
- Citing in presentations to ensure acknowledging source content using an oral medium

Chapter Objectives

After reading this chapter and completing the exercises, you will be able to:

- Differentiate between APA and MLA source acknowledgement styles.
- Explain errors in reports to avoid making error in source acknowledgement.
- Analyze source content to determine its feasibility for use.

Many official documentation and citation formats are available. Several are industry driven. For example, journalists use the Chicago Manual of Style or the AP Stylebook. Compare source acknowledgements in journal articles and news articles. You will notice that in-text acknowledgements are placed in articles. For example, according to the Associated Press, "According to" is called a signal phrase. The source does not appear in parentheses, as an in-text parenthetical citation in journal articles. This is because the style standards are different as each type of document is different.

Students and academics usually use the Modern Language Association (MLA) style. Professional writers, scientists, and researchers usually use the American Psychology Association (APA) style. No matter the style, each dictates the proper way to credit sources. This section will provide examples of citation and documentation of various types of sources for two of the most popular formats: MLA and APA.

You must include identifying elements, such as the name of the author and/or editor, the title of the source, the name and primary location of the publisher, and the publication date.

What is consistent across MLA and APA documentation styles is the placement of the author's name (or authors' names). The name is the first entry in the documentation. However, punctuation and capitalization differ, as well. For example, in MLA format, the author's last and first names are spelled out. In APA format, the author's last name is spelled out; the author's first initial is used. Regardless of the documentation style, you want to follow its format standards. MLA and APA use in-text parenthetical citations.

For APA format, when the signal phrase contains the name of the source, the in-text citation contains the year the source was published and the page number. Note: When a page number is not included, include the paragraph (para.) number; for example, (1997, para. 4).

Remember that you must include in-text citations and the documentation page; you cannot have one without the other. Be sure that the citations and documents match up. One without the other results in an important piece of a puzzle being lost. You want to guide the reader directly to the source.

Each source, from an article to a book, a chapter, an editorial, or a website, has its own documentation and citation format. Here are examples of sources that you may use to support your thesis. This list is not an all-inclusive list, but rather a sampling of the most common sources.

Hardcopies

A book with one author

MLA Works Cited

Darley, Gillian. *Vesuvius*. Cambridge, Mass.: Harvard University Press, 2012. Print.

APA References

Darley, G. (2012). *Vesuvius*. Cambridge, MA: Harvard University Press.

A book with more than one author

MLA Works Cited

Ember, Carol R., Ember, Melvin R., and Peregrine, Peter N. *Anthropology*. New York: Prentice Hall, 2010. Print.

Example in-text citation: (Ember, Ember, and Peregrine 82).

For more than three authors, it is unnecessary to list them. Instead, include the first author and the notation et al., which is Latin for *and others.*

Example in-text citation: (Ember et al. 35).

APA References

Ember, C. R., Ember, M. R., & Peregrine, P. N. (2010). *Anthropology.* New York, NY: Prentice Hall.

For more than two authors, it is unnecessary to list them. Instead, include the first author and the notation et al, which is Latin for *and others.*

Example in-text citation: (Ember et al., 2010, p. 82)

Ember et al. (2010, p. 82) states…

A book edited and revised by another author

MLA Works Cited

Strunk, William. *Elements of Style.* Ed. E. B. White. 50th Anniversary ed. New York: Pearson Longman, 2009. Print.

APA References

Strunk, W. White, E. B. (Ed.). (2009). *Elements of Style.* New York, NY: Pearson Longman.

An edited collection

MLA Works Cited

Miller, Susan, ed. *The Norton Book of Composition Studies.* 1st ed. New York: W. W. Norton & Company, 2009. Print.

APA References

Miller, S. (Ed.). (2009). *The Norton Book of Composition Studies.* New York, NY: W. W. Norton & Company.

An essay that appears in an edited collection

MLA Works Cited

Christensen, Francis. "A Generative Rhetoric of the Paragraph." *The Norton Book of Composition Studies.* Ed. Susan Miller. New York: W. W. Norton & Company, 2009. 283–296.

Example in-text citation: Christensen has developed a nine-pronged approach to the structural analysis of a paragraph (284).

Note: If the author's name were not included in the paraphrase, you would have to include it in the in-text citation. Example: (Christensen 284).

APA References

Christensen, F. (2009). *A Generative Rhetoric of the Paragraph*. In S. Miller (Ed.), The Norton book of composition studies (pp. 283–296). New York, NY: W. W. Norton & Company.

Example in-text citation: Christensen has developed a nine-pronged approach to the structural analysis of a paragraph (2009, p. 284).

A business pamphlet

Often, business pamphlets and brochures will not have a name attached to them. These works are considered collective since they represent the company, not an individual. Therefore, the first entry is the name of the company, organization, or association.

MLA Works Cited

Search Institute. *Your Workplace Simple Investment, Big Reward*. Minneapolis: Search Institute, 2004. Print.

In-text citation example: Adult employees expect confidentiality and clearly written documents ("Your Workplace" 8).

APA References

Search Institute. (2004). *Your workplace simple investment, big reward* [Pamphlet]. Minneapolis, MN: Author.

In-text citation example: Adult employees expect confidentiality and clearly written documents ("Your Workplace" 2004, p. 8)

A government pamphlet

MLA Works Cited

United States. Eastern National. *Castillo San Felipe del Morro*. San Juan, P.R., 2008. Print.

Note: For governmental documents in MLA format, begin with the country. In this case, Puerto Rico is a U.S. territory, not an official country. Eastern National is the organization that sponsored the pamphlet. Castillo San Felipe del Morra is the name of the National Historical site. Next is the location, date of publication, and publication form.

In-text citation example: For more than 250 years, the Spanish Empire protected El Morro ("Castillo San Felipe del Morro").

APA References

San Juan National Historic Site. (2008). *Castillo San Felipe del Morro*. San Juan, P.R.: Eastern National.

In-text citation example: For more than 250 years, the Spanish Empire protected El Morro ("Castillo San Felipe del Morro," 2008, para. 1).

An article from a reference book (encyclopedia, for example)

MLA Works Cited

"Gibbs, Mifflin W. Judge and United States Consul." *International Library of Afro-American Life and History*.1978. Print.

APA References

Gibbs, Mifflin W. Judge and United States Consul (1978). In *International library of Afro-American life and history*.

A Poem or short story in a book

MLA Works Cited

Dunbar, Paul Laurence. "To The Memory of Mary Young." *The Complete Poems of Paul Laurence Dunbar*. New York: Dood, Meand and Company, 1913. 81. Print.

APA References

Dunbar, P. L. (1913). To the memory of Mary Young. The *Complete Poems of Paul Laurence Dunbar*. New York, NY: Dood, Meand and Company.

A letter to the editor

MLA Works Cited

Geist, Kathie. "A 'Civil' Past of Racism?" Editorial. The Christian Science Monitor 19 Mar. 2012: 32. Print.

APA References

Geist, K. (2012, March 19). A 'civil' past of racism? [Letter to the editor]. *The Christian Science Monitor*, p. 32.

A book review

MLA

Kafka, A. C. "Accordion File." Rev. of Squeeze this! A Cultural History of the Accordion in America by Marion Jacobson. *The Chronicle of Higher Education The Chronicle Review* 30 Mar. 2012: B15. Print.

APA

Kafka, A. C. (2012, March 30). Accordion File [Review of the book *Squeeze this! A Cultural History of the Accordion in America*]. *The Chronicle of Higher Education The Chronicle Review*, p. B15.

Daily newspapers article:

APA References

Reese, T. (2012 May 27) Try to avoid 'Siphoning off your 401(k). *Harrisburg Patriot-News*, p. B2.

MLA Works Cited

Reese, Tom. "Try to Avoid Siphoning Off Your 401(k)," *Harrisburg Patriot-News* 27 May 2012: B2. Print.

A website

APA References

USGS: Science for a Changing World (2012 May 2). *U.S. Geological Survey.* Retrieved from http://www.usgs.gov/

MLA Works Cited

United States. Geological Survey. *Science for a Changing World*. U.S. Geological Survey. 2 May 2012. Web. 28 May 2012.

Note: Begin with the author or business author of the site. *Place the name of the site here.* Place the name of the sponsor here. Include the date of publication or date of last update. Place the date accessed here.

An online version of a book

MLA Works Cited

Baldwin, Mary Alice. *The New England clergy and the American revolution*. Hathi Trust Digital Library. n.d. Web. 29 May 2012.

APA References

Baldwin, Mary Alice. *The New England clergy and the American revolution.* Hathi Trust Digital Library. Retrieved from http://catalog.hathitrust.org/Record/000363625.

An online article

MLA Works Cited

Light, Nathan. "Genealogy, history, nation." *Nationalities Papers* 39.1 (2011): 33–53. Web. 29 May 2012.

APA Works Cited

Light, Nathan. (2011, January). Genealogy, history, nation. *Nationalities Papers.* Retrieved from http://web.ebscohost.com.ezproxy.hacc.edu/ehost/pdfviewer/pdfviewer?vid=3&hid=10&sid=45501b74-b6ef-4bca-8671-40ef7e69fe8a%40sessionmgr14

An e-mail

You may find it necessary to conduct primary research electronically. Here is how you would cite the information.

MLA Works Cited

Jones, Sharon. "Role of Department Chairs." Message to the author. 15 Apr. 2011. E-mail.

APA References

Note: An APA References entry is unnecessary because APA does not acknowledge personal, irretrievable information. However, you would have to include an in-text citation.

For e-mail messages sent as discussion group or list serve, Milton, M. (2012, May 22). Webinar for recruiting, managing and leveraging the millennials in your business [Message posted to GoToAssist mailing list] Retrieved from http://www.citrixonline.com

A blog in its entirety

MLA Works Cited

Sonya Hubbard. Rite Aid gets another frequent flyer stamp… Footnoted. 29 May 2012. Web. 29 May 2012.

APA References

Sonya Hubbard. (2012, May 29). Rite Aid gets another frequent flyer stamp…
[Web log post]. Retrieved from http://www.footnoted.com/

An essay in an online collection

MLA Works Cited

Korshin, Paul J. "Johnson, the essay, and The Rambler." The Cambridge Companion to Samuel Johnson. Ed. Greg Clingham. Cambridge University Press, 1997. *Cambridge Collections Online*. 26 February 2012. Web.

Exceptions for APA References

You have the option of using the URL (universal resource language) or the DOI (digital object identifier) to lead the reader back to the original source. The DOI is a new identifier that was designed to allow for permanence to a source; thus, making it easier for users to find a source over time. If you include the URL, you do not have to include the DOI.

Korshin, P. J. (1997). Johnson, the essay, and The Rambler. In G. Clingham (Ed.), *The Cambridge Companion to Samuel Johnson.* doi:10.1017/CCOL052155411X.005

Not all sources will have complete information. For example, a date and name of the author may not appear. This is especially the case for online sources. Although some formats indicate the lack of this information (n.d. for no date), you may want to reconsider using the source. Remember that reliable sources have complete information. Complete information is the first category for ensuring a valid source.

> Application: Review the Works Cited pages for this textbook. Are there any sources with an n.d. notation? If so, comment on the reliability of the source(s).

You may come across sources that have no page numbers or the page numbers may change due to pagination differences. Should this be the case, you can indicate the paragraph, screen, or section number. These categories will not change; all systems and users will have the same number. For paragraphs, count the paragraph in which the quote, summary, or paraphrase resides. For MLA, use the abbreviation par for paragraph (pars for plural); sec for section (secs for plural); or screen (screens for plural). Example: (Hollins, screen 2)

Differences between MLA and APA—At a Glance

MLA	APA
Use the word Web to indicate an internet source. However, if your professor requires the URL, you must include it.	Use URL or DOI.
Use the authors' full name.	Use the author's first name initial and complete last name.
List primary research in-text and Works Cited page.	List primary research in-text only.
Use the source's complete name.	Omit articles, even if they are part of the name. (Change "The American Lung Association" to "American Lung Association.")
Use *and* when listing more than one author.	Use an ampersand when listing more than one author.

Sample Works Cited Page

Works Cited

Korshin, Paul J. "Johnson, the essay, and The Rambler." The Cambridge Companion to Samuel Johnson. Ed. Greg Clingham. Cambridge University Press, 1997. *Cambridge Collections Online*. 26 February 2012. Web.

Light, Nathan. "Genealogy, history, nation." *Nationalities Papers* 39.1 (2011): 33–53. Web. 29 May 2012.

Search Institute. *Your Workplace Simple Investment, Big Reward*. Minneapolis: Search Institute, 2004. Print.

Sample References Page

References

Baldwin, Mary Alice. *The New England clergy and the American revolution.* Hathi Trust Digital Library. Retrieved from http://catalog.hathitrust.org/Record/000363625.

Darley, G. (2012). *Vesuvius.* Cambridge, MA: Harvard University Press.

Geist, Kathe. "A 'Civil' Past of Racism?" Editorial. The Christian Science Monitor 19 Mar. 2012: 32. Print.

Gibbs, Mifflin W. Judge and United States Consul (1978). In *International library of Afro-American life and history.*

Light, Nathan. (2011, January). Genealogy, history, nation. *Nationalities Papers.* Retrieved from http://web.ebscohost.com.ezproxy.hacc.edu/ehost/pdfviewer/pdfviewer?vid=3&hid=10&sid=455 01b74-b6ef-4bca-8671-40ef7e69fe8a%40sessionmgr14

Putting the Writer, Source, Text, Citation, and Documentation Together

A recommendation report proposes solutions to solve work-related problems. The following report, *Interpretive Services in Health Care*, was written by a student in a business communication course. Specific points[1] are highlighted. As you read the report, write additional comments pertaining to how the writing moves from writer to source, signal phrases, in-text citation format, and the references page format.

Interpretive Services in Health Care

its

Gateway Health Plan has a concern with their participating provider's refusal to offer interpretive services for their racial and ethnic minority patients. Gateway Health Plan services the medical assistance and Medicare/Medicaid dual eligible population. Physicians and hospitals are required to provide interpreter services to patients under Title VI of the Civil Rights Act of 1964. Practices are reluctant to provide interpreter services due to the high costs and are requesting patients to bring their own interpreter. By bringing their own interpreter, many times children, create a bigger break-down in communication which ultimately means the patient is not receiving excellent quality of care.

Identify the problem

Comment on the relationship between the problem statement and purpose.

WHY WRITE A REPORT?

The purpose of this report is to recommend options for physicians and their staff in providing interpretive services to their racial and ethnic minority patients. It will focus on the quality of patient care, errors in patient care due to poor or lack of interpretive services and identify specific methods of interpretive services available. If the Provider Relations Representatives can provide detailed information on the importance of providing interpretive services it will help increase the quality of care, and will reduce preventable illness and deaths.

For healthcare organizations to continue providing the highest quality care to all of their patients, they must implement culturally competent services within their organizations. While there are no national standards for providing culturally competent care, many excellent policies exist. The International Medical Interpreters Association says an interpreter's primary task is to transform a message in a source language—the health care provider's language—into its equivalent in a target language—the patient's. (Link, 2006)

Comment on whether this citation supports the paragraphs that proceed it.

WHAT WILL THE REPORT COVER?

This report will show the importance in providing interpretive services to their patients. Quality of Care is of the upmost importance today, the understanding of medical care between the patient and the physician. The risks involved by using a child or family member with limited English or understanding of medical terminology can be devastating to the patient's health. With regard to services available, this report will look at several ways to manage quality of care through education, and interpretive services.

Investigate whether this is a formal term to determine whether capitalization is necessary.

WHAT WILL NOT BE COVERED IN THIS REPORT?

This report will not provide specific costs associated with interpretive services. Costs and services vary with each interpretive service organization and program. Costs associated with the different types of services vary as the services can be provided by phone, internet, electronic devices or a computer application programs.

Comment on how discussing topics that are not included in the report increase the writer's credibility.

WHAT ASSUMPTIONS WERE MADE?

The assumption is that a huge percentage of providers are not providing interpret services to their patients. When the patient calls to schedule an appointment and does not speak English or has limited English skills they are asked to bring an English speaking, family member or friend with them to their appointment. Additionally, the assumptions are made that if good interpretive services were in place for their patients' their quality of care would increase. Therefore their patients would be healthier,

List examples that appear throughout the report that support this assumptions.

Describe the academic honest impact should the writer not address the assumptions in the body of the report.

Revise this sentence to improve grammatical structure.
understand their health, and play a role to ensure they are following their physicians care appropriately.

WHERE DID THE INFORMATION COME FROM?

Comment on whether the writer can discuss research in third person instead of first person. If so, rewrite these sentences.

The information from this report comes from my discussion with Evonne Allen, Director Provider Relations at Gateway Health Plan, and Center for Disease Control (CDC), and several publications; magazines, and journals. This information helped in my search by giving me facts and data previously researched, and surveys on the issue of language barriers. Material also comes from my eleven years of experience in provider relations, and twenty-five years in the insurance industry.

WHAT CRITERIA WERE USED TO EVALUATE IDEAS?

Describe the information that must appear in the body of the report to support these points.

The criteria used to assess the recommended options consist of educating physicians and their staff on the importance of health care disparities, and implementing effective interpretive services techniques to safeguard racial and ethnic medical care. Using a child or family member can and does impact poorly on the patient's health through the breakdown in communication. This is an issue in the majority of cases because the interpreters have little knowledge of health-care terminology or they are too young to understand the significance of accurate translation.

Percentage of Racial and Ethnic Minorities

Comment on the correctness of citations is this section. Make any changes to make it academically acceptable.

Many surveys have been conducted over the last few decades regarding the language barriers with racial and ethnic medical care. The Center for Disease Control (CDC) conducted a race and ethnic health surveillance survey in 2000 to monitor chronic disease and behavioral risk factors. The health care community agrees that reducing racial and ethnic disparities in healthcare is extremely important. The goal is to improve or implement programs to improve health conditions in the racial and ethnic patients with such chronic conditions as cardiovascular, diabetes, and hypertension. In addition, it is important to conduct preventive screenings for such things as colon and rectal cancer, gonorrhea, and chlamydia.

The study found that areas with high numbers of racial and ethnic minorities, as well as linguistically isolated households participating in the survey were significantly lower. Controls were then added to educate the Spanish speaking population in the health study; however the education created no increase in participation.

The U.S. Census Bureau shows from 1980 to 2002 that the proportion of minorities among the civilian, noninstitutionalized population grew from

6.4% to 13.3% among Hispanics, 11.7% to 13% among blacks, and 1.5% to 4.4% among Asians. The U.S. Census also shows that 11.7% of United States citizens were born in a foreign country. The percentage rates are expected to show a continued increase each year.

Evidence shows that there is a continued growth in people who speak a primary language other than English. The 2000 U.S. Census recorded 18% of people aged five and older spoke a language other than English at home. This percentage increased three percent from 1980 to 1990.

The communication between physician and the racial ethnic minority patient is essential to quality of life and health care. More than ever physicians need to ensure they have open communication with their racial ethnic patients. Racial and ethnic minority patients must be able to convey their medical needs and/or concerns to their physician in order that they receive appropriate care.

The first graph shows the percentage of Hispanic or Latino Adults aged 18 years and older.

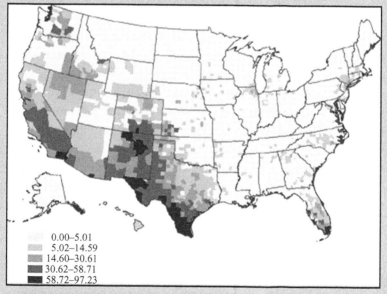

0.00–5.01
5.02–14.59
14.60–30.61
30.62–58.71
58.72–97.23

Source: U. S. Census 2000

The second graph indicates the percentage of Asian or Pacific Islander adults aged 18 years and older.

In terms of introducing a source, what is this sentence an example of?

Comment on the strength of this paragraph as a prelude to source information. Offer suggestions for improving it.

Offer suggestions for how the writer can explain the source information and put it in context for the reader.

Explain how the reader can incorporate more of her writing.

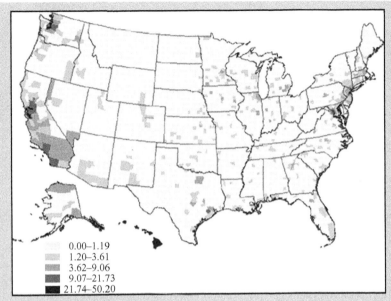

```
0.00–1.19
1.20–3.61
3.62–9.06
9.07–21.73
21.74–50.20
```

Source: U. S. Census 2000

HOW DID WE GET HERE?

The problem with racial and ethnic disparities has been an ongoing issue for many decades. The United States government first admitted the issue existed in 1999. The government hired the Institute of Medicine to conduct an independent study of disparities in health care among racial and ethnic minorities. The Institute of Medicine is an independent non-profit organization who reports the gold standards for health-care policymakers.

Explain why this word is inappropriate for a report.

The study resulted in a shocking outcome. The study uncovered an overwhelming concern in racial and ethnic patients receiving lower quality standards of care in their healthcare regardless if health insurance or income was considered. They were more likely to die from a treatable chronic condition, less likely to receive medications and surgical procedures.

Explain the connection between these paragraphs. Include suggestions for connecting the writer's commentary with the source notation.

Healthcare disparities are still a challenge today. It is still unclear what is causing many of the disparities. Additionally, if the issues were identified we are not sure how to act upon the concern and decrease them. Historically physicians were trained to treat all patients the same. We are learning that different races and ethnicities can't be treated in the same manner. For example, diabetes rates higher in African Americans and Hispanics than in whites.

Almost all common health issues have two root causes: the "nature" ones and the "nurture" ones, which come from one's environment. For minority health issues, both categories are complicated. Race is a notoriously inaccurate proxy for genetics, since it's such an imprecise way of describing people. (Carmichael, 2010)

How to Break the Disparities Barriers

I searched many articles, journals and websites for the best practices for physicians to utilize when treating their racial and ethnic patients. I found numerous discussions on this issue with a few successful hospitals/physicians who by providing interpretive services for their racial and ethnic patients are providing excellent quality of care.

Comment on how the writer can strengthen information on all primary and secondary research.

EDUCATING PHYSICIANS AND HOSPITALS

Physicians and their staff need to be trained and educated on healthcare disparities with their racial and ethnic minority patients. They need to understand the importance of adequate and understandable conversations with their patients' about their health. Taking the time to understand their needs at point of service will improve their health and reduce healthcare costs.

Based on the heading, list three to five areas the writer should include to support this section.

In addition to the need to improve the technical components of care, there is a need to improve interpersonal aspects of care, improve cross-cultural interactions and communication, and increase patients' involvement. All providers must be trained to improve their cross-cultural interpersonal interactions to engage patients from all racial and ethnic diversity of health care providers need to be increased.

Training health care providers to improve cross-cultural interactions can reduce disparities in those interpersonal components that result in greater patient satisfaction, engagement, and cooperation with health care regimens. Such training can target all health care providers, particularly physicians and their staff.

MEDICAL INTERPRETER IN-HOUSE

Hospitals are recognizing not only the need for interpreters for their racial and ethnic minority patients but they need to understand their beliefs, religion, where they come from and how they live their lives. Translating is not enough in treating these patients.

As a provider relations representative I visited an office last year where an office manager shared a story with me. This particular patient falls in the racial and ethnic category. She would arrive for her appointment

List the details the writer needs to provide to support primary research.

before the office even opened. The staff didn't understand why she was doing this so they tried shifting her appointment times around so that she wouldn't have to sit in the office all day. After several attempts at trying to accommodate this patient and telling her she didn't have to come so early the doctor had a conversation with the patient. The next time the patient arrived she brought a picture with her. This pictured showed a small old building with men, women and children waiting in a long line. As it turns out, where she was from you didn't make an appointment it was "first come first serve".

Physicians that are not part of a Physician Health Organization (PHO) or work for a physician owned hospital should look to their local hospital for interpreter services connections. Working together is beneficial to both the physicians and hospitals in improving the healthcare disparities for racial and ethnic minority.

ELECTRONIC INTERPRETIVE TOOLS

Offer suggestions for phrasing this section in third person instead of first person.

Comment on the support for this suggestion, based on the data presented.

Suggest another way to present this information.

Google Translator is free and translates for sixty-five languages. Some examples of the languages needed in our area are; Chinese, Japanese, Spanish, Russian and Italian. I asked several medical questions to ensure the appropriate translation. Here are some of the questions I asked; have you had your mammogram? We will be giving you a flu shot today, and can you show me where the pain is located? In each instance the translation was completely accurate. In addition, I did a reverse translation to ensure it was correct both ways, English to Chinese and Chinese to English.

Most all physician offices today have computers and/or laptops which would allow them to utilize this free and accurate Google application. By using some type of electronic device to assist with racial and ethnic minority patients the physicians and staff might even begin to learn some of their language.

Summing up the Choices

Comment on the support supplied for these three research points.

By using a collaboration of education, joining forces with local hospitals for interpretive services, and using free electronic tools Gateway's participating physicians can raise the needle in quality healthcare. Racial and Ethnic disparities are still an ongoing issue across the United States. Best practices will continue to be developed; physicians will be required to learn more about health care disparities and how they can make a difference. Together as a country we can work to improve the health of our United States citizens.

References

Beal, A. C. (2004). Policies to reduce racial and ethnic disparities in child health and health care. *Health Affairs, 23*(5), 171–179. https://ezproxy.hacc. edu/login?url=http://search.proquest.com/docview/204624141?accoun tid=11302

Carmichael, Mary. "Why Racial Disparities in Health Care Persist." *The Daily Beast.* Newsweek/Daily Beast, 14 Feb. 2010. Web. 11 Apr. 2012. <http://www. thedailybeast.com/>.

Larson, L. (2009). Word for word, culture to culture. *Hospitals & Health Networks, 83*(7), 44–45, 1. https://ezproxy.hacc.edu/login?url=http://search. proquest.com/docview/215294469?accountid=11302

Link, Michael W. PhD. (2006, January 1). *Preventing Chronic Disease.* Retrieved April 15, 2012, from Centers for Disease Control: http://www.cdc. gov.pcd.issues/2006/jan/05_0055.htm

Phillips, K. A., Mayer, M. L., & Aday, L. A. (2000). Barriers to care among racial/ethnic groups under managed care. *Health Affairs, 19*(4), 65–75. https://ezproxy.hacc.edu/login?url=http://search.proquest.com/docview/204 495412?accountid=11302

Tennant, S. (2010). Targeted population studies needed to reduce health disparities. *Managed Healthcare Executive, 20*(12), 23–24. https://ezproxy. hacc.edu/login?url=http://search.proquest.com/docview/845260312?accoun tid=11302

Wolf, E. J. (2001). Providing culturally appropriate care: A tale of two hospitals. *Healthcare Executive, 16*(2), 12–17. https://ezproxy.hacc.edu/ login?url=http://search.proquest.com/docview/200312721?accountid

Identify the formatting errors on the References page. Rewrite the page using the correct format.

[1]*Interpretive Services in Health Care* by Kimberly Hammond, April 12, 2012. Written for Business Communication course at Harrisburg Area Community College, spring 2012.

Annotated Bibliography

Justifying your sources is important not only to the reader, because it provides credibility to your analysis; it also helps you to associate the source with your topic.

An annotated bibliography is a list of sources that you used or will use in a report. Each citation is followed by a brief (approximately fifty words) descriptive and evaluative paragraph, known as the annotation. The purpose of the annotation is to inform the reader of the relevancy, accuracy, and quality of the sources cited. The writing style that you project is expository. Here are some suggestions for composing the annotated bibliography.

Suggestion One

Read the article, and summarize it aloud, as if you were explaining it to a classmate. It will be helpful to record your explanation on your iPad, iPhone, or any electronic device. Find the main premise of the article. Explain the main premise, and support it with data presented in the article. Compose the annotated bibliography based on your oral explanation.

Suggestion Two

Read the article, and write the main points in your own words. Determine how you would use the information in your report. Compose the annotated bibliography based on its value to the report.

The following example uses the MLA format for the online journal citation:

Lands, B. and Lamoreaux, E. "Using 3–6 differences in essential fatty acids rather than 3/6 ratios gives useful food balance scores." *Nutrition & Metabolism* 9.46 (2012): n.p. Web. 24 May 2012.

Researchers have confirmed that the consumption of foods high in fatty acids decrease the occurrences of diseases and illnesses. Foods rich in omega-3 and omega-6 convert theses acids into hormones that help the body fend off diseases. The article analyzes the omega 3–6 food scores to determine the best food choices and prescription drug choices to prevent and/or maintain cardiovascular disease.

You may be required to present the results of your research. The following section provides details or oral citing and documenting acknowledgements.

Citing in Presentations

Citing and documenting are essential, regardless of the communication medium. Any information that you quote, summarize, or paraphrase on a presentation screen (or recited during the presentation) must include in-text citations (written or oral) and a References or Works Cited Page. The documentation page can be one of the handouts you provide to your audience.

As a presentation screen with an in-text citation appears, explain the significance of the information and recite the source. Here is a presentation screen for the student recommendation report that appears in this chapter.

For this source, what information would you include to support it? Other than stating, "This map comes from the 2000 U.S. Census," how could you emphasize the importance of the information from this source? What would you say to introduce the source? How would you explain the numbers represented by the source? Compose a script for presenting this map. Refer to the student's complete report in Chapter 3, Part I.

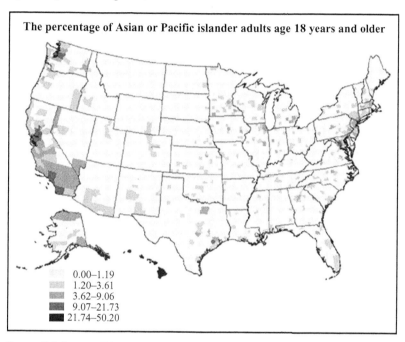

The percentage of Asian or Pacific islander adults age 18 years and older

0.00–1.19
1.20–3.61
3.62–9.06
9.07–21.73
21.74–50.20

Source: U. S. Census 2000

Proper Citing of Experiments

When conducting experiments based on previous research, you must acknowledge the inventor of the experiment. This is also the case when replicating experiments to determine whether the results are valid today as they were, for example, sixty years ago. Or, perhaps you want to alter the experiment parameters a bit to make it pertinent to present day. Whatever the case may be, you are beginning with an original experiment based on someone else's idea, concept, or data. Therefore, you must acknowledge the originator of the experiment, and you must explain the alternations you made and why you made them.

Summary

Honest Reflection: Describe a plan that will help you put your writing, sources, text, citations, and documentation together.

Works Cited

Hammond, Kimberly. *Interpretive Services in Health Care*. ENGL 106 Written Communication (Professor Valerie A. Gray). Harrisburg Area Community College. 12 Apr. 2012. Print.

Exercises and Application
3.1 Write an Annotated Bibliography

Find two hard copy sources and two electronic sources on an academic topic of your choice that you will compose into an academic or professional research paper. Write an annotated bibliography for each source.

3.2 Practice Citing, Documenting, Verifying, and Incorporating

This exercise provides you with the opportunity to develop your writing by supporting it with sources. Read the following article, *Bed Bug (Cimex lectularius L.) Population Composition as Determined by Baited Traps*. You can find the article at the doag.org website. Begin with synthesizing the information by writing a thesis/problem statement. Is there common knowledge that you can add to the discussion? If so, include it in the problem statement to support the topics for discussion. Next, determine three points for the report's focus. Conduct additional research by finding one other source that is listed on the References page. Write a one-page discussion on the topic.

3.3 Writers' Commentary: Avoid Research Fallacies

Here are examples that could appear in written documents or via conversations at the water cooler. Identify the solutions to keep the fallacy from appearing in the text. What portions of the statement do not make sense? What information should the writer have included to avoid the fallacy? Rewrite the example to illustrate your solutions.

Fallacy	Definition	Example	Solutions	Revision
Ad hominem	Belittling the person or topic with which you disagree, and ignoring the issues at hand	Dr. Wilson does not know about herbal medications because he is a quack.		
Appeal to popular opinion	An all-inclusive statement that does not take into account varying points of view	Everyone agrees that the data are correct.		
False analogy	Support for a subject by comparing it to a subject that is totally different	The bailout of the auto industry will fail because Enron went bankrupt.		
False cause	Establishing a cause and effect between two things without connecting the relationship	Egyptian art and African art have the same characteristics.		
False dilemma	Stating that there are only two options while not presenting other alternatives	The marketing department must either hire three new employees or continue to see a decline in productivity.		

Fallacy	Definition	Example	Solutions	Revision
Hasty generalization	Drawing a conclusion from a sample/sample group that is too small or segmented	Two of twenty-one employees completed the survey. They both agreed that the graphics department needs to increases its production budget by 30%.		
Ignoring the burden of proof	Presenting no evidence to support a claim	Requiring that the human resources coordinator obtain his HRIM will improve his communication skills.		
Red herring	Concentrating on an issue that has nothing to do with the topic	If the vice president reorganizes the division, we can have more compensatory time per year.		

Information overload can led to fallacies; therefore, choosing reliable sources is important to substantiate your thesis.

3.4 Your Task—Highlighting Your Writing

As a writer, you are close to your composition. This attachment can sometimes make it difficult to determine where your knowledge ends and a source's concepts begin. Here is an activity that will help you categorize your writing and visualize how you have incorporated your text with source information.

You will need:

- The draft of the text that you think is ready to turn in to your instructor or supervisor
- Five highlighters; one each in blue, pink, yellow, green, and orange

Proofread the draft. With the blue highlighter, identify your writing—transitions, details, and signal phrases. With the pink highlighter, identify all quotes. With the yellow highlighter, identify all paraphrases. With the green highlighter, identify all summaries. With the orange highlighter, identify all in-text citations.

Closely examine your draft. Did you include the required in-text citations? Does your writing encompass most of the paper? Did you correctly identify the sources? Was the majority of the text, 75%, written by you? If so, you are ready to turn in the paper. Submit your highlighted version, with your sources, and a clean copy of the paper to your instructor.

If not, you will have to repair all problem areas. Repairing it may mean that you will have to conduct more research, learn about the topic, and incorporate more of your writing.

3.5 Unit Review

What is APA an abbreviation for?

What is MLA an abbreviation for?

What is the purpose of using MLA and APA?

What is the purpose of research writing?

What is paraphrasing?

What is summarizing?

What is quoting?

What does the following in-text citation represent?

The critic Susan Hardy Aikens has argued on behalf of what she calls "conanical multiplicity" (qtd. In Mayers 677).

Is it necessary to cite the following information: One of four high school students will not receive a diploma. Be prepared to support your answer.

Part Two

Writing to Establish Your Information Literacy Reputation

Information literacy pertains to your ability to understand where to find reliable sources, how to set criteria for using a source, and how to determine the best sources to use for objective, correct, and concise information.

Chapter Four focuses on writing for your profession. This chapter describes the ethical code of conduct that workers in a profession are expected to uphold. Working solitarily within a business is very rare; therefore, this chapter presents case studies to help you determine whether it is necessary to cite sources if using secondary internal business documents. Chapter Five presents definitions and criteria for information in the public domain and information that is copyright, registered, and trademarked.

Part Two, therefore, serves as an informative orientation to and application of professional situations because it describes regulations and protections against information infringement. Additional assignments appear at the end of the chapter.

CHAPTER 4

Business Integrity Standards

As presented in Part One, ethics is what underlies academic and business honesty standards. Integrity and ethics are characteristics that define your professional reputation. Agencies such as the Society for Technical and Scientific Communication, Institute of Electrical and Electronic Engineers (IEEE), and the Society for Business Ethics are just a few of hundreds of organizations that regulate and present codes of conduct for professionals regarding integrity, confidentiality, and professionalism. Each profession has an ethical code of conduct. Ethical code of conduct refers to moral and ethical expectations that organizations want members and workers to follow as they complete their workplace obligations.

These organizations have bylaws that define how information is conveyed internally and externally. For example, the American Historical Association (AHA) includes a section on plagiarism in its bylaws. Members of AHA have included this subject to ensure ethical behavior for its membership.

> All historians share responsibility for defending high standards of intellectual integrity. When appraising manuscripts for publication, reviewing books, or evaluating peers for placement, promotion, and tenure, scholars must evaluate the honesty and reliability with which the historian uses primary and secondary source materials. Scholarship flourishes in an atmosphere of openness and candor, which should include the scrutiny and public discussion of academic deception. (Statement on Standards of Professional Conduct)

The topic of plagiarism and ways to avoid it will always be important, regardless of your field of study or what you want to do as a profession.

To what professional organization do you belong?
What is its stance on plagiarism or copyright infringement?

Companies may adhere to rules of the business ethics; others may not. Even though a defining organization may set the code of conduct for its body, what happens if your supervisor advises you that, for the purpose of a report you are preparing, you do not have to worry about intellectual infringement or your supervisor tells you "this is the way it has always been done." What would you do? After all, you like your job, you receive good pay, and it may be difficult to get another job. You do not want to rock the boat or upset your supervisor. You want to stay under the radar. Perhaps these are the internal conversations you may have if you are ever faced with ethical dilemmas. Thinking about how you will handle such situations will help you make the ethical choice under pressure.

Collective Writing

Business documents, such as a letter or memo, will include the writer's name. However, other business documents usually will not include the writer's name. Ownership does not rest with the writer but with the company. Many times, documents are written collectively, meaning several employees will collaborate on a writing project. This is particularly true when a document exceeds 100 pages, when the document contains several topics, or when the document must be completed under a strict deadline.

Each document that a company produces is considered a legal document. Information is gathered from employees within the organization, from past documents, and through primary and secondary research. Although the act of writing may be individualistic, the recognition for the writing is collective.

Is it necessary to document internal sources? Explain your answer.

To examine an example of a collectively written business document, visit http://www.ppi.noaa.gov/wp-content/uploads/BOM.pdf

---

Case Study: Correspondence from Pacer Systems. Can the original document be used?

Sarah is the new Human Resources Coordinator for Pacer Systems, Inc. Her job entails writing correspondence to employees explaining their benefits, informing them about wellness initiatives, and coordinating family and work initiatives. As a new employee to the department, she wants to ensure continuity in the way information is presented. She understands the importance of corporate culture and wants to ensure a comfortable transition for employees as they develop a relationship with her.

Sarah's boss, Meredith Jones, suggested that she review the archives of department correspondence over the past twenty years. For legal purposes, the department archives company correspondence.

Sarah's first correspondence is a light, fun topic to bring employees together. She is informing them of a luncheon the H.R. department is sponsoring for all employees. She reviewed the memos to develop a tone appropriate for the organization. She came across a few memos that she thought were good examples of the style she wanted to project. The content is similar: an H.R. – sponsored picnic.

Sarah knew she had to revise some typos and grammatical errors, for example, errors in noun/pronoun agreement. Other than making these corrections and changing the date and location, she did not see the need to change the style and content of the memo.

Sarah represents the company, the department, and herself. Her name appears on the From: line. If she makes minimal changes, has she completed her task? Describe the steps Sarah should take to compose a document that represents her style.

Proprietary Data

Proprietary refers to confidential or private business information that is disseminated to select employees within the organization. These employers usually sign nondisclosure contracts and have a security clearance. Depending on the industry, revealing proprietary data can lead to arrest. Often, employees must maintain the confidentiality of the information, even when they leave the organization, ensuring that they will always uphold ethical codes of conduct. And, of course, they do not want to break the law. Examples of proprietary information include ingredients to a recipe, formulas, blueprints, computer codes, and national security. The company owns the rights to this information. Companies have proprietary clauses to ensure a competitive edge.

What are some possible downsides to companies securing proprietary data?

Malcolm Gladwell, author of *Outliers* and *The Tipping Point*, wrote an article for *The New Yorker* entitled "Creation Myth" in which he theorized the convergence of innovation among high-profile employees at Xerox PARC, an offshoot of Xerox Corporation and Apple. Go to http://www.gladwell.com/2011/2011_05_16_a_creationmyth.html to read the article. Gladwell questions the notion that any innovation is truly created; the entrepreneurial creation involves change, not creation, and ownership is abstract. Therefore, claiming proprietary status is difficult. After you read the article, write a one-page, single-spaced response addressing his thesis. Provide support for your position.

From a business position, proprietary information is recognized by three symbols: copyright, register mark, and trademark.

Copyright©

Copyright refers to a literary, artistic, technological, or other type of authorship that has exclusive legal rights for the holder of the copyright to distribute sale, produce, or reproduce the object. It is the discretion of the holder of the copyright to grant permission to produce, reproduce, or sell the object.

Examples of copyright material:
  Books
  Lyrics
  Poems
  Plays
  Scripts
  Pantomimes
  Choreography

Source: US Copyright Office

The originator of the material must seek a copyright to serve as protection from copyright infringement.

The originator of the material must register the work through the US Library of Congress, pay for the registration, and receive licensure. If the originator agrees to let someone use all or a portion of the copyright material, he/she can receive payment.

Registered® Mark

The registered mark supersedes the trademark; it is the final step to proprietary status. The United States Patent and Trademark Office (USPTO) assigns the registered mark to an object when it has been registered. For the best protection of intellectual property, an object receives the registered mark.

Trademark™

Businesses that want to be identified by a product, name, symbol, mantra, or saying will seek legal recognition, protection, and ownership through registration known as trademark. An infringement of a trademark refers to a company or individual using the exact or similar name, symbol, or mantra, so much so that it would cause confusion among consumers. (Premiere Trademark™).

Words, symbols, and icons are so associated with brands that all we have to see is the symbol or icon. For example, consider the sneaker that has a symbol that resembles a check mark, or the red and yellow M for a fast-food restaurant. These symbols are registered trademarks.

Information Considered Public Domain

Recently, the patent on Lipitor, a statin drug that scientists say reduces harmful cholesterol levels, allowed for competitors to produce similar and generic statins. This opened marketing and advertising.

Exclusivity, which the Food and Drug Administration (FDA) grants, allows pharmaceutical companies to advertise and market drugs for six years within the patent, or not. Exclusivity opens competition between generic drug providers and drug creation. (Source: Frequently Asked Questions on Patents and Exclusivity http://www.fda.gov/Drugs/ DevelopmentApprovalProcess/ ucm079031.htm#How%20 many%20years%20is%20a%20 patent%20granted%20for?)

Service Mark

An object can receive a service mark (sm) to indicate that the United States Patent and Trademark Office (USPTO) is investigating whether a request for, or implementation of, proprietary production already exists for the same item.

Patent

A patent protects ideas or inventions.

The patent holder has limited ownership of the patent. A patent expires twenty years after the completion of the patent application (Patent Terms and Extensions). The holder can sell the patent and not receive any royalties, or the holder can keep it and receive any income from it. If you describe patented ideas, you must include the patent number and the name of the owner of the patent.

Identify Five Examples of Information for Which You Must Include The Copyright Symbol in Your Document.	Identify Five Examples of Information for Which You Must Include The Registered Mark in Your Document.
1.	1.
2.	2.
3.	3.
4.	4.
5.	5.

List three examples of trademark information.

1.

2.

3.

For more information on copyright, registration mark, and trademark, visit:

http://www.uspto.gov/

http://www.uspto.gov/patents/resources/general_info_concerning_patents.jsp#heading-2

Corporate Cultural Influence

Corporate culture encompasses the acceptable norms, conduct, expectations, and traditions that a company portrays. Corporate culture is the way in which a company operates. It is reflected in the way employees dress (conservative, casual, or casual Fridays); the way employees address their supervisor (first name as opposed to title, or surname); off-site activities (parties, picnics, social gatherings); proximity of supervisor to employees (the supervisor in an office

What Is Your Definition of Professionalism?

Who sets the rules? Many companies set their own rules and definitions for professionalism. Corporate culture shapes your perception of a company. Visit Organizational Culture at http://managementhelp.org/organizations/culture.htm for information on various categories of corporate culture.

at one end of the hall, while employees are at the opposite end in cubicles). It also involves the way information is written and disseminated to employees and stakeholders (customers, clients, agencies, regulators). Corporate culture can reinforce or circumvent professional codes of conduct.

Writing Articles from Information in a Press Release

A press release is a short, one- or two-page document announcing an event, an innovation, or a change in personnel. Depending on the news, the popularity of the company, and the consumer base, a company will send the release to local, regional, or national media outlets. These outlets use the release to determine whether to announce the information to the public. A release is not detail driven. The reporters for the media outlets use the release to compose questions and to seek additional details. Reporting only the information on the press release is akin to reporting only the abstract of a journal article.

The company that sent the release is the primary source. The reporters will conduct additional primary research via interviews and other primary research to establish the necessary background and historical significance to contextualize the information for the public.

Press releases tell the basics; they answer the how, who, what, where, when, and why. The front-end of the release begins with specific information and funnels downward to general details. This funnel is known as the inverted pyramid.

Practice writing an article based on a press release. Go to http://www.fda.gov/NewsEvents/Newsroom/PressAnnouncements/default.htm. This site

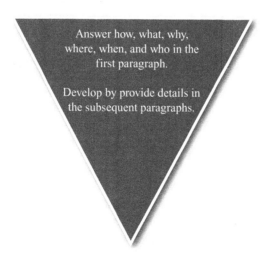

Answer how, what, why, where, when, and who in the first paragraph.

Develop by provide details in the subsequent paragraphs.

contains a myriad of releases from the Food and Drug Administration. Choose any release that interests you.

Compose seven open questions that you want to explore in drafting an information article for the general public. You must compose a question beginning with one of the adverbs or pronouns presented in the inverted pyramid. From your research questions, conduct primary research. Note: This is the only type of source that you can use. Press releases will have the contact information of the person responsible for disseminating the press release. Contact the company and other knowledgeable sources. It is always a good idea to obtain opposing points of view because doing so will strengthen the credibility of the article.

When discussing business integrity, the discussion is not limited to words. Images are also included. The following section describes how using open visuals can pose problems for the image of businesses.

Using Stock Visuals

Stock visuals are images that are available for use; however, don't require users to seek permission from the owner. The most famous images represent cliché business or familial situations. There are numerous open-source visuals on the internet that are not copyright; therefore, they do not need the owners' permission. Sites such as shutter.com or Microsoft© allow users to download photographs, clip art, symbols, and templates for formatting documents. For Microsoft, as the purchaser of the license to use the software, you may use the templates, symbols, clip art, and photographs to format information. The format does not need citation; only the text from which the formatting is based.

Stock Visuals and Multiple Representations

Many companies want to project an image of inclusiveness and diversity in the workplace and its clientele. Often, stock photos are used as a marketing device to heighten this image. A brochure for Bank of America and a website for Citi Group displayed the same picture of an African-American couple contemplating their financial future.

Key Bank and Bank of America used the same familial image of a father working on his laptop and his daughter looking over his shoulder. (Source: Steel, Emily. "When Marketers See Double; As Digital Libraries Spread The Use of Stock Photographer, Some Ad Images Are Recycled." *ABI/Inform Research*. Wall Street Journal, 28 Nov. 2006: B.1. Web. 10 Mar. 2012.)

Stock photos make copying easy and acceptable. When a company uses stock images, it lowers the level of originality, making it difficult for each company to develop a unique visual image marketing brand.

Websites such as shutter.com. iStockPhoto.com, and freephotosbank.com offer stock photos free or for a minimal charge. These sites are royalty free; users do not have to pay a fee for every time a photo is used.

Many companies do not have internal photographers; therefore, they outsource to stock photo providers. It costs pennies to purchase a photo. However, to hire a photographer, arrange for models, and secure a location for the photo, it can costs thousands of dollars (Steel B.1).

Company icons such as pictures and logos communicate much to stakeholders. You are probably familiar with the truism, "a picture is worth a thousand words." Company pictures communicate an image to stakeholders. Visuals serve as a nonverbal interpersonal communication vehicle for companies. But what happens when various companies use the same images? Similar to common knowledge, common imagery is available for use by anyone. This is a rather common way to communicate information. Does commonality make this practice more acceptable? What can companies do to be more original in image design and decrease costs?

> Ethical Reflection: Identify an ethical concern for stakeholders and their interpretation of stock images.

There is a difference between photos provided by stock providers and photos in the public domain. Public domain authors and photographs grant permission to use without a fee. Users of photographs from stock footage companies usually have to pay a one-time fee as a licensure.

Regardless of the source type, it is necessary to cite the source. Here is the documentation style.

APA

Name of artist or creator (Type of artist). (Year the picture was taken). Title of picture in italics [Type of art], Retrieved Full Date, from: URL.

When you know the title but not the artist, cite a stock photograph in APA style like this: Title of picture in italics [Type of art]. (Year the picture was taken). Retrieved Full Date, from: URL.

When you do not know the artist or the title, cite a stock photograph in APA style like this: [Description of picture and type of art]. Retrieved Full Date, from: URL.

MLA

Name of artist or creator. *Title of the work of art*. Date the image was created. *Database Name or Title of the Site. Web.* Date of access.

Note: For stock photos and public domain images, it may be difficult to find the name of the artist or creator. Should this be the case, begin with the title or caption of the photograph.

Are You Seeing Reality?

Photographs have been manipulated for more than 100 years. The changes range from subtle to overt. Even without the use of Photoshop, it is difficult to determine the change to the original photo. The website Four and Six Photo Tampering throughout History lists photos and descriptions of how they were manipulated. Visit:

http://www.fourandsix.com/ photo-tampering-history/ to view the manipulations.

Manipulating Visuals

Manipulating visuals, or visual distortion, involves changing the appearance of the original visual. Visual manipulation can range from cropping a photo to illustrate a particular portion that pertains to your text, to juxtaposing an image onto the original photograph, deleting a portion of the original photograph, or using Photoshop or another software package to alter the image. The word *manipulation* has a negative denotation. Manipulation means to influence for one's own advantage or benefit. This manipulation can be done unethically, for example, to provide a biased view of the data or to persuade the reader to focus on a particular segment of the visual.

Think of the manipulations to visuals in the same way you think of manipulations to text: any manipulation without informing the reader is unethical because what you are presenting is not the original. Pulling out a portion of the photo to focus on particular point can be done to emphasize a point; however, does the story or impression change if you do so? Are you trying to hide information from the reader? Regardless, you must indicate that you manipulated or changed the image. Before the visual appears in a document or presentation, introduce it and explain any alterations you made and why you made them. It is important to let the reader know up front before examining the visual. After the visual appears, explain its significance to your research.

Works Cited

American Historical Association. *Statement on Standards of Professional Conduct.* 8 June 2011. Web. 28 Feb. 2012.

Cross Law LLC. *Trademark Basics.* Premiere Trademark™. 2009. Web. 8 June 2012.

Free Management Library. *Organizational Culture.* 2000. Web. 8 June 2012.

Steel, Emily. "When Marketers See Double; As Digital Libraries Spread The Use of Stock Photographer, Some Ad Images Are Recycled." *Wall Street Journal* B.1 (28 Nov. 2006): B.1. Web. 10 Mar. 2012.

United States. *Copyright in General.* Library of Congress. United States Copyright Office, 28 Feb. 2012. Web. 28 Feb. 2012.

United States. *Frequently Asked Questions on Patents and Exclusivity.* United States Department of Health and Human Services, 9 Aug. 2011. Web. 2 Mar. 2012.

United States. *2700 Patent Terms and Extensions.* United States Patent and Trademark Office. n.d. Web 2 Mar. 2012.

Part Three

Sampling from Popular Culture

Popular culture is influencing society more than ever. Technological advances, such as tablets and smart phones, and social media sites have made electronic communication almost as instantaneous as face-to-face communication. New media, a term applied to ways in which information is disseminated electronically, has also made communication and information literacy essential, as information changes from one moment to the next. With such immediacy, it can be difficult to determine what information is reliable and what information is gathered through the grapevine of social media.

Chapter Five describes how art forms other than writing are susceptible to being plagiarized; thus, such art forms must be cited and documented. These art forms include music, graffiti art, fine art, kitsch art, and YouTube videos.

You will notice more photographs are used in Chapter Five. This technique highlights the influence of pop culture in issues of fair use and accusations of plagiarism.

Part Three, therefore, serves as an exemplification of how new media infuses various voices. Questions, textboxes, and activities appear throughout the chapters to help you develop strategies for analyzing popular culture sources and incorporating new media sources. Additional assignments appear at the end of Chapter Five.

CHAPTER

5

Annotate Contributors

New media has made collaborative writing more convenient than ever before. However, with convenience comes responsibility. With the infusion of various voices, it can be difficult to determine authorship. This chapter presents ways to determine individual contributors, determine the reliability of a contributor, acknowledge the original source that produced the new media, and recognize how art influences ownership of ideas. This chapter presents the idea that many artists believe: using other contributions is an homage, similar to a tribute or recognition of the power and influence a person, place, or thing has. This chapter also presents information to discuss whether these contributors and artists are violating rules of ownership, citation, and documentation.

Chapter Objectives

After reading this chapter and completing the exercises, you will be able to:

- Define sampling and tagging.
- Understand the importance of questioning information obtained via social media.
- Understand the need to cite and document information from social media.
- Understand the obligation the researcher has in documenting information from social media.

Art that Samples the Original

Some say the highest form of flattery is imitation. This saying is reflected in an art term known as reworking, in which an artist takes an original piece of work and changes it. The artist is taking artistic license, which is a term used to describe when an artist is given the liberty to interpret another artist's work.

Figure 5.1 Margaret Garner

Artists create images that are influenced by other works of art. For example, Pulitzer Prize winning author Toni Morrison was inspired to write the novel, *Beloved* based on a picture drawn by Thomas S. Noble in 1867. The drawing entitled "Margaret Garner" depicts a runaway slave who escaped to Ohio. However, because of the Runaway Slave Act, owners from a slave state, in this case Kentucky, could cross state lines and capture their slaves, even if the slave had escaped to a free state. Rather than return her daughter to a life of bondage, Margaret Garner killed her child. The story of Margaret Garner is a true.

> Ms. Morrison took a historical event and used it as a basis for her fiction work. Did she commit plagiarism?

Inspiration versus Duplication

Popular culture (pop culture) and pop icons are people, places, and things that are defined as entertaining and known to be influential to a large segment of a population. The influence of the pop icons can be due to negative or positive events. The event can be current or past. Examples of pop culture icons include Elvis, Jimmy Hendricks, Michael Jackson, Justin Beiber, the Kardashians, *Survivor*, and *American Idol*.

Brian Donnelly, also known as KAWS, coined the phrase "original fake," which is part of the domain name for his retail website (http://www.original-fake.com/). KAWS is known for his iconic rework of pop culture originals such as Mickey Mouse, the Michelin Man, the Smurfs, *SpongeBob SquarePants*, and *The Simpsons*.

The original image is distinct; it is easy for the audience, who is familiar with these pop icons, to understand the inference, or allusion. The Michelin Man has been promoting tires since 1898. *The Simpsons* has been on television for over twenty years, first starting as vignettes on the HBO original company show *The Tracey Ulman Show*, and then appearing on the Fox network for more than twenty years. Mickey Mouse was introduced on November 14, 1928. *Mickey's Follies*, an animated film, appeared in 1929. The Smurfs have been in production in one form or another for more than fifty years. The first episode of *SpongeBob SquarePants* aired on May 1, 1999. KAWS' reworking does not distort the image so that it is unrecognizable.

> The images appear in the book *KAWS: 1993-2012* by Brian Donnelly, New York: Skira Rizzoli: Aldrich Contemporary Art Museum, 2010.

A tag is an attachment or marking on an object that identifies it as new or different. Tagging has negative connotations when it describes graffiti because many critiques believe graffiti is not art. Also, when graffiti artists tag the art of another artist, it is seen as a sign of disrespect. KAWS takes iconic pop culture images and tags them with symbols and shapes, changing the image, its function, and its meaning.

Is Parody Free from Acknowledgement?

A parody is an imitation, usually initiated by comedians and satirists, to ridicule the works of an artist or pop culture icon.

Depending on the parody, the comedian or satirists will have to clear permission to alter the original. For example, comedian Weird Al Yankovic is known for his parodies of popular music. Recently, he wrote a parody of Lady Gaga's hit, "Born This Way" and changed it to "Perform This Way."

According to postings on his blog, Weird Al Yankovic stated that he contacted Lady Gaga to let her know his intent, even though he believed this parodies fall under fair use laws. However, Lady Gaga denied his request. To read Weird Al's viewpoint, visit http://alyankovic.wordpress.com/the-gaga-saga/

At the time, Lady Gaga's denial prevented Weird Al from releasing an album that included the parody. However, Weird Al did post his song on YouTube. To hear "Perform This Way" visit http://www.youtube.com/watch?v=fUxXKfQkswE

Imitate and Borrow

Image © s_bukley, 2012. Used under license by Shutterstock, Inc.

Image © Helga Esteb, 2012. Used under license by Shutterstock, Inc.

If you borrow, should you have to return that which was borrowed? If you watch any of the reality shows in which a pop culture judge decides the outcome of the case, the answer is no; the loaner should have no such expectation. However, in the real world in which most of us function, if you borrow, you need to repay the loaner via a form of acknowledgement—citing, documenting, or paying a permission fee.

> What is the irony in Lady Gaga being involved in a permission of use dispute with Weird Al Yankovic?
> (Note: You will have to tap into your allusions and pop culture knowledge.)

Is it possible for choreographer to plagiarize a dance? Beyonce and her artistic director were accused of borrowing moves. Read the opinion piece, and ponder the questions that appear throughout it.

Image © arvzdix, 2012. Used under license by Shutterstock, Inc.

In Dance, Borrowing Is a Tradition

ALASTAIR MACAULAY

The "Nutcracker" season is almost upon us—but can you be sure who choreographed all of the versions you might see? Last year, as I toured the United States in a "Nutcracker" marathon, I observed how more than 12 American productions featured the Sugar Plum pas de deux that Lev Ivanov choreographed for the 1892 original in St. Petersburg. But in only one case was the pas de deux—whose adagio, early on, features a beautifully spectacular phrase unlike anything else in 19th-century ballet, with the ballerina seeming to peel herself open in her partner's arms—actually credited to Ivanov.

Should we call this plagiarism? I ask because, in October, the choreographer Anne Teresa De Keersmaeker observed that Beyonce and her director, Adria Petty, had lifted sequences from two of Ms. De Keersmaeker's works, "Rosas Danst Rosas" and "Achterland," in a recent video, "Countdown." Thanks to the use of close-ups on screen, Beyonce's borrowings look unmistakable.

Ms. Petty, moreover, in an article on GQ.com, said of Ms. De Keersmaeker, "Her work blew my mind." She added that she regretted that, because video editing had been so rushed, that Ms. De Keersmaeker was not given a credit.

She said, "And the hope from my end was that this would put her work out there in front of a lot of people who wouldn't have discovered it otherwise."

Ms. De Keersmaeker's first reaction was to say: "This is plagiarism. This is stealing." She later conceded, "I am glad that 'Rosas Danst Rosas' can perhaps reach a mass audience, which such a dance performance could never achieve, despite its popularity in the dance world since 1980s."

I'm afraid I can't get exercised about the subject: Ms. De Keersmaeker's simple movements are scarcely of striking originality in the first place. The way Beyonce and Ms. Petty have chosen to fill the screen with them makes the parallel far more intense than it would appear onstage. But then, Ms. De Keersmaeker's choreography follows the tradition of many postmodern choreographers in being concerned not with original movements but with recontextualizing ordinary ones. We aren't wrong, as a rule, to consider George Balanchine among the most original of choreographers—yet we can also see why he liked to stress the other side. When people praised him as a creator, he'd say, "God creates—I assemble." Assemblage, not invention, is the choreographer's basic task.

Compared with the chunks of unacknowledged Ivanov in multiple American "Nutcracker" productions, the Beyonce/De Keersmaeker issue is peanuts. Several of those Sugar Plum pas de deux I saw around the country also featured sequences from Balanchine's 1954 version, which is danced by New York City Ballet and at least four other American companies. It's now marketed as "George Balanchine's 'The Nutcracker'"—yet at least two important parts of it aren't by Balanchine. He made no secret about having taken his Nutcracker Prince's mime scene and the Candy Cane number (the hoop dance to the Russian trepak music) from the version he had danced in Russia in his youth.

The program acknowledgments, however, tend to pass over this. At least two other ballets listed in New York City Ballet's repertory as "by Balanchine"—"Pas de Dix" and "Minkus Pas de Trois"—feature whole sequences and dances almost entirely by Ivanov's senior contemporary Marius Petipa. If you're in ballet-sleuth mode, you should also take notice of a favorite Balanchine device: to take some well-known steps from the original and set them to another part of the music. In "The Nutcracker" he takes the most famous step of the original 1892 Sugar Plum Fairy, the gargouillade (a sideways jump in which the feet write rapid rings in the air)—whole series of them—and gives it instead to the ballet's third-ranking female figure, the Marzipan dancer, who performs it to different music.

These liftings—far more sizable than Beyonce's—recur often in ballet. If you're steeped in various versions of "The Sleeping Beauty" and go to Peter Martins's version at City Ballet, you can actually tell, when it comes to the solo that Princess Aurora dances as a vision in Act II, which video Mr. Martins was looking at when he staged his version in 1991. The first three-quarters of his solo come, step for step to the same music, straight out of the Royal Ballet version, as broadcast in 1978. They were in fact the work not of the ballet's first choreographer, Petipa (who chose not to set this part of Tchaikovsky's score, and whom Mr. Martins acknowledges as one of his sources), but by the Royal Ballet's founder-choreographer, Frederick Ashton (whom Mr. Martins doesn't acknowledge), in 1952. Since Mr. Martins changes the dance's ending, however, he can say that it is his own spin on received material.

Is this a big deal? Probably not. Ashton in turn began this dance by adapting Petipa steps here to different music. He also placed into almost all his ballets a phrase that he had seen Anna Pavlova dance. He changed its dynamics, its duration and some of its internal details so as to keep its reiteration a secret from the audience. (Even when you know how it goes, it can take you many dozens of viewings to spot some of its occurrences.) Though his dancers called it "the Fred step," Ashton himself told me he meant it as a Pavlova talisman, a private acknowledgement to her inspiration.

One famous choreographer who did cry "Thief!" was Jules Perrot, the best-known ballet choreographer of the mid-19th century. In 1861, on the charge of "infringement of copyright in choreography," he took to court none other than Petipa, then in the early stage of his long career. Petipa had arranged a one-act ballet, "Le Marche des Innocents," for the

Paris Opera debut of his wife, Marie Petipa. It had music by Cesare Pugni, who had composed for both Perrot and Petipa. Marie Petipa asked Perrot, who had also arrived in Paris that summer, if she could dance his "pas" (dance) "La Cosmopolitana" (originally arranged for his ballet "Gazelda, ou Les Tsiganes") within her husband's ballet. Perrot had said no; the Petipas used it anyway.

The 1861 court ruled in favor of Perrot, agreeing that the composition of a dance "could nevertheless constitute a composition in which copyright might exist." Even though this pas had been performed first in Russia, it was the work of a Frenchman, and so copyright applied in France. Perrot was awarded 300 francs damages.

Had Ms. De Keersmaeker's lawyers tried taking Beyonce to court, they would have had a far weaker case; the Perrot-Petipa dance was one unbroken dance with identical music, whereas Beyonce's very short snippets are danced to her own score. As it is, Ms. De Keersmaeker's reputation has only been improved. Has Beyonce's been damaged? Scarcely. We can call her a pilfering magpie without finding her less watchable.

There would be better legal ammunition in all those "Nutcracker" productions. But the reasons few have wasted time crying, "Thief! Thief!" about the choreography of Ashton, Balanchine and so many regional "Nutcracker" stagers are obvious. Those works contain their thefts, but they contain greater signs of assemblage.

Application: There is a citation and documentation format for just about every type of artistic expression. Find the MLA format for dance and provide an entry applicable to the article.

Usher versus Homer Simpson

In a 2003 Christmas episode of *The Simpsons*, Homer Simpson sings his excitement about Christmas. The lyrics and music are not profound; however, they are at the center of a lawsuit against singer, Usher Raymond. The creators of *The Simpsons* have accused him of plagiarizing Homer's Christmas ditty through his recording of OMG ("Wait, Wait, Don't Tell Me").

Image © catwalker, 2012. Used under license by Shutterstock, Inc.

Image © Featureflash, 2012. Used under license by Shutterstock, Inc.

For a side-by-side comparison of the two versions, visit http://www.you-tube.com/watch?v=xgCo5DVX3XQ

For addition information on the suit, visit

http://www.dailymail.co.uk/tvshowbiz/article-1342196/Did-Usher-plagiarise-Homer-Simpson-R-B-star-accused-stealing-Springfield-stars-song.html#ixzz1lLX4ubVF

Describe your response to the lawsuit. What similarities and differences do you hear? Is this an example of plagiarism?

Sampling an Original

Sampling in music is the incorporation of previously recorded music and/or lyrics of one artist with the lyrics, music, and/or rhythms of a DJ or rapper to produce new music (Schloss).

Remixing through electrical production is an example. Does a musician who samples committing copyright infringement or is he just expressing himself creatively; is he using creative license?

Assignment:

Michel Foucault (1926–1984) is considered one of the most influential European intellectuals of the twentieth century. (Norton 1615). In his manifesto, "What Is an Author?", one topic he addressed was authentication and attribution. For Foucault, authors not only compose their text, but also "the possibility and the rules of formation of other texts" (1632 The Norton Anthology of Criticism and Theory). Think about this quote as you read Mickey Hess's article, "Was Foucault a plagiarist? Hip-hop sampling and academic citation." You can access the article via http://www.mickeyhess.com/hessfoucault.pdf.

Write a three-page response to Hess's article. Specifically, present an analysis of the author's attainment of his goal to "juxtapose sampling with academic citation to determine their shared values of responding to sources" (282). Comment on how understanding sampling, citation, and documentation will help you develop ownership and empowerment by owning your writing. How does Foucault's position on Marxism and capitalism shape his view of plagiarism? How does Foucault's approach fit in real-world situations (academic and business).

Sampling is used most notably in rap music with interesting, unique, and creative pairings. For example, you may be familiar with the rapper Jay-Z song "Hard Knock Life," released in 1998. You may be more familiar with the Broadway musical, *Annie* in which the song "Hard Knock Life" is one of many memorable songs. Jay-Z samples the verse, using children to sing the verse to mimic the orphans singing in the original version.

Jay-Z did receive permission to use the lyrics in his song; however, he received permission under false pretenses. It is true that Jay-Z felt a personal connection with the lyrics of "Hard Knock Life." In his memoir, *Decoded*, he stated that, "… Annie's story was mine, and mine was hers, and the song was the place where our experiences weren't contradictions, just different dimensions of the same reality" (240). Jay-Z wanted to sample the song. When Jay-Z's lawyer initially contacted the lawyers of publisher to obtain permission for use, he was denied. In an effort to circumvent the decision, Jay-Z tried another tactic. He wrote a letter to the copyright holder explaining why using the lyrics is important to him. The letter explained that when he was in the seventh grade, he won an essay contest. His prize was a trip to Broadway to see the musical *Annie*. He stated that from that moment, he connected with the story Based on his passionate letter, he was granted permission. However, the story isn't true (240).

To hear the original Broadway production of "Hard Knock Life, visit,

http://www.youtube.com/watch?v=6UIiT6ry6zQ

www.youtube.com/watch?v=ahdBUnVEuYM

To hear Jay-Z's sampling, visit,

http://www.youtube.com/watch?v=zxtn6-XQupM

How would you classify Jay-Z's approach to securing permission of use? Should he be required to pay for use retroactively? Defend your answer.

New Media that Infuses Various Voices

New media encompasses internet-based communication via social technology such as blogs, Twitter, wikis, podcasts, Facebook, and YouTube. New media allows users to communicate virtually in real-time conversations, follow "friends," and share information.

Blogs

A blog is an electronic diary or journal that the blogger (writer) can share with millions of readers. A blog can discuss one's personal thoughts and opinions, offer medical advice, offer life advice, share recipes, sports, and comment on political views, just to name a few. In addition to text, bloggers can upload photographs and videos. Bloggers can be reporters, experts in the blog subject matter, and average citizens with opinions about a subject, with no subject expertise. Any subject you can think of, there is probably a blog for it.

How can you tell a blog is from a reliable source? It is important to distinguish between facts and opinions. The criteria for measuring the reliability of a blog is the same as the criteria you should measure for a web page. Investigate the credentials of the person hosting a blog. The blog should have a byline to inform the reader of the person and publisher responsible for the information. Refer to Chapter Three for APA and MLA documentation format for a blog.

Twitter

The author of tweets has 140 characters, including spaces, to communicate her message. This allows tweeters to post short information to followers (readers) of tweets, allowing them to track the activity of their family, friends, or favorite pop culture icons. Think of tweets as small talk that would occur in face-to-face conversations. Followers can sign up to receive the tweets of their favorite pop culture icons, company products, and the latest headline news. The most talked about tweets are those from entertainers such as Kim Kardashian and Ashton Kutcher. Media outlets and businesses use Twitter to communicate headlines and new products. There are more than 200 million accounts on Twitter ("Twitter").

Ethical Reflection
When citing new media:
- Determine individual contributors.
- Determine open source venues.
- Acknowledge the original source when posting and incorporating YouTube videos.

The formats for tweets are new, as this social medium is being cited more and more. The following APA format comes from a blog entitled, How to Cite Twitter and Facebook, Part II: Reference List Entries and In-Text Citations, published by Chelsea Lee.

APA Format

BarackObama. (2009a, July 15). Launched American Graduation Initiative to help additional 5 mill Americans graduate college by 2020: http://bit.ly/gcTX7

During a tour of national parks in 2011, GOP 2008 presidential vice presidential nominee Sarah Palin concluded her experience following her visit at the Paul Revere house by explaining Paul Revere's midnight ride. Her explanation was not clear, and she misspoke about the facts.
Palin supporters changed the entry for Paul Revere on Wikipedia to reflect her interpretation of history and Paul Revere's Midnight ride.

[Twitter post]. Retrieved from http://twitter.com/BarackObama/
status/2651151366

Here is the order of information in a tweet: The name of tweeter. (Date of tweet). Title of tweet. URL of tweet.

MLA Format

Butner, Scott. "Honey bee hovering." 10 June 2012, 9:14 p.m. Tweet.

Last name, First name of tweeter. "Title of tweet." Day month year of tweet, time of tweet. Tweet.

Wikis

Wikis are collaborative online writing environments in which various users can comment on and change the thesis of the literary work. The most used wiki is Wikipedia. Wikipedia is a collaborative online encyclopedia that pulls together the information from contributors for the public domain (Knobel and Lanshear, p. 17).

Why do many instructors forbid students from using Wikipedia as a source for research papers?

What is the best function of Wikipedia for information literacy?

YouTube

YouTube is official known as an online repository. Think of YouTube as a library of home videos, travel videos, television shows, movies, and instruction, which are searchable and accessible in the public domain.

How to Cite YouTube Videos

APA Format

Jay-Z. *Hard Knock Life*. (Date of video). Retrieved 2012, May 6 from http://www. dailymotion.com/video/x1hh1w_jay-z-hard-knock-life_music

In-text (Jay-Z, year of posting)
(Jay-Z, 2007)

MLA Format

Jay-Z. "Hard Knock Life." *YouTube*. Access on 6 May 2012. http://www.dailymotion.com/video/x1hh1w_jay-z-hard-knock-life_music

In-text ("Hard Knock Life")

Understanding Academic Honesty from a Cultural Perspective

Thus far, you have learned about corporate culture and popular culture and their influence on academic and professional honesty. It is important to consider how your culture influences your academic and professional standard. You are a member of various cultures. You have your familial culture, your ethnic culture, your gender culture, and your club organization culture, just to name a few. You are born into a culture, and you learn cultural values. Although outer cultures will influence your individual culture, ultimately, your individualistic approach is what will lead you to do all that you can to avoid plagiarism.

Culture is divided into two categories: high context and low context. High context refers to countries in which information is shared sparingly or incompletely. One way to determine whether a country is high context or low context is to examine its government and media. If its government or media is considered a democracy and is, for the most part, open to sharing information and sending alerts to consumers, it is low context. Contrarily, if the government and media only give partial information, one-sided information, or no information, it is considered high context.

High-context cultures tend to be collaborative societies, meaning any recognition to the group or family structure is given as a whole, not to individual members within the group or family. Low-context cultures value individual achievement and recognition.

> **Ethical Reflection**
> As you know, if you write a paper and commit plagiarism, you could receive a variety of punishments; either you will fail the paper, fail the course, or be suspended/expelled from the university. If you are a member of a collaborative group and one member commits plagiarism, your professor may punish each member. This is because the assignment guidelines were set up to be collaborative; each group member is responsible for reviewing sources and signing off on the assignment before turning it in.
> When you write individually and collaboratively, it is your individual responsibility to ensure the work is correct.

In some cases, students from high-context cultures may devalue their writing and believe compiling sources is a collaborative writing style. They believe compiling shows more respect to the original sources. However, students who compile instead of write are doing a disservice because they are not learning to write in an academic and professional style. You must take due diligence in understanding your sources to write and document thoughtfully and concisely. Remember: To comprehend a topic, you must understand 95% of the words (www.lextutor.ca/research/).

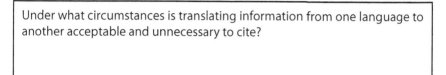

Under what circumstances is translating information from one language to another acceptable and unnecessary to cite?

Under what circumstances would it be fair and acceptable to use culture as an excuse for academic dishonesty ignorance?

Social media make our lives more convenient and instantaneous. We can access information within seconds. To a certain degree, because of this convenience, our encounter with the information appears to be personal and, thus, it is easy to claim ownership. However, as you have learned, it is important to be conscientious about the decisions you make regarding when to correctly and effectively take ownership and authenticity of your writing with honesty and integrity.

Works Cited

Carter, Shawn (Jay-Z). Decoded. Spiegel & Grau: New York. 2010. p. 240.

Chelsea Lee. How to Cite Twitter and Facebook Part II: Reference List and In-Text Citations. APA Style. 26 Oct. 2009. Web. 29 May 2012.

Cobb, Tom. *Why & how to use frequent lists to learn words.* Vocab Research Resources. n.d. Web. 30 Mar. 2012.

Darley, Gillian. *Vesuvius.* Cambridge, Mass.: Harvard University Press, 2012. Print.

Foucault, Michel. "What is an Author?" *The Norton Anthology of Theory and Criticism.* Ed. Vincent B. Leitchr. New York: W. W. Norton & Company, 2001. 1632.

Knobel, Michele and Lankshear, Colin, eds. *A New Literacies Sampler.* 1st ed. New York: Lang Publishing, 2007. 17. Print.

Leitch, Vincent B., ed. *The Norton Anthology of Theory and Criticism.* 1st ed. New York: W. W. Norton & Company, Inc., 2001. 1615. Print.

Leitch, Vincent B., ed. *The Norton Anthology of Theory and Criticism.* 1st ed. New York: W. W. Norton & Company, Inc.,2001. 1617. Print.

Nobel, Thomas. *Margaret Garner.* 1867. National Underground Railroad and Freedom Center, Cincinnati. ARTstor. Web. 23 Mar. 2012.

Schloss, J. G. *Making beats: The art of sample-based hip-hop.* Hanover, CT: Wesleyan University Press, 2004. Print.

"Twitter." *New York Times Business Day.* 19 Dec. 2011. Web. 26 Mar. 2012.

"Wait, Wait, Don't Tell Me." National Public Radio. 2 Jan. 2011. Radio.

Weird Al Yankovic. *Lady Gaga-Saga.* 12 June 2012. Web. 29 May 2012.

Exercises and Application Assignment 5.1

Response to Paraphrasing in Art

Your instructor will place *KAWS: 1993–2010* on reserve at your library. Choose three KAWS re-works, one of which must be the billboard for Met Life with Snoopy and Woodstock in a plane. For each artistic piece, answer the following questions:

How does artistic license differ from a writer's license to use sources to his or her artistic discretion? Why can't you claim artistic license when you write a paper and decide to compile your sources?

Is an artist who reworks infringing on copyright, trademark, or plagiarizing? Provide a 150 to 200 word response.

Assignment 5.2
Connecting with a Popular Culture Source to Explore Social Themes

Choose a social theme that emerges in "Hard Knock Life." Compose a strong thesis to support a 500-word commentary of the theme. Find one reliable source with statistical data that you must use to support your commentary. Of course, include a Works Cited page with your commentary.

Assignment 5.3
Analyzing Tweets for Accuracy and Reliability

Find three tweets that you think are reliable. Should you need a refresher on reliability measurements, refer to the tips in Chapter Two. Identify why you think they are reliable. Identify how you could use the tweets in a research paper. How would you put the tweets into complete context for the reader? Explain each tweet in no more than 140 characters.

Exploring Culture Differences and Perceptions of Academic Honesty

In your sociology class, you have decided to write a paper on intercultural communication styles in high-context countries. You decide to search SocINDEX with Full Text database because it contains articles on cultural studies. You realize that the topic "intercultural communication" is too broad. You know that you will have to first establish a concrete research topic. Your multiple tasks include:

Write a Concrete Topic

Find two articles from two different journals and authors that address the topic.

Write a one-page response to each article that details how each author treats the subject, any contractions and similarities, the credentials of the authors. Be sure to write an introduction that explains the purpose of the response and a conclusion that summarizes your analysis.

Write a Research Paper

Write a three-page paper on how the perception of plagiarism in another country. You may choose the country. For this assignment, conduct primary research. For example, you can interview a friend, co-worker, classmate, instructor, etc., who is from another country and knowledgeable about the subject. Write at least ten open questions about the topic. Note: The questions must be new and add to the discussion on the topic.

- Outline the organization of the paper.
- Identify whom you will interview.
- List your questions.
- List the two sources you will use and explain why they are being used (annotated bibliography).
- Use APA format for sources.

Analyzing Sources

Go to http://www.academic-journals.org/ojs2/index.php/IJCSE/article/viewFile/531/16 to read the article, Website Design Guidelines: High Power Distance and High-Context Culture. From the References listing, choose three sources. For each source, indicate where you found it. For each of the three citations you identified, write an annotated bibliography; write a paragraph for each source that identifies its use in the article. Explain how it supports or does not support the authors' text.

Conduct research on the source that is referenced. What is the author(s) credentials? What makes him/her an expert in the field?

Designing an Assignment

What type of project or assignment can you present that would involve using sources from the National Archives and media collections? Design an assignment in which you would use these sources to support your text. Explain the assignment, the type/location of the sources from the National Archives. The assignment and location of the media collections. Why are these sources so valuable to your assignment? What knowledge would you bring to the assignment?

Applying Inductive Logic, Deductive Logic, and Hypothesis

It is important to know the "old school" way of researching. This assignment requires you to find information at an actual library. You may ask a librarian to assist you.

Narrow a research topic that is of interest to you for each of the following categories. Compose two research questions per topic:

- Cultural
- Critical
- Historical
- Societal

Be sure to compose questions that reflect critical thinking skills. For examples, the answers to the questions must be readily found or easily answerable. Here are the steps to get you started:

- Develop a list of open research questions.
- Write active voice signal phrases.
- Write an outline for a research paper.
- Write an annotated bibliography.

The Rules to Avoiding Plagiarism—FAQ

1. My instructor did not tell me that I had to cite sources. Am I still obligated to do so?

    If you used information from sources, you must include in-text citations and a documentation page; it does not matter whether an instructor told you to do so or not. If your professor did not tell you to cite, he or she probably thought that this fact does not need to be overly stated. You want to always maintain academic honesty; be proactive without being prompted.

2. Many times, instructors will give open-book exams. Can I take information directly from the book and present it as my answer?

    No. The purpose of an open-book exam is to spark your memory so that you can formulate answers on your own. The purpose is not for you to regurgitate information presented in a textbook. Doing so does not foster learning; it fosters imitation. Should you regurgitate information, you should expect your professor to record an F as your grade.

3. How do I know what I know?

   Before you begin researching a topic, write down everything you think you know about it. You can always verify facts that you think you know. If those facts are easily verifiable, you do not have to cite the source. If you cannot verify the information, you must conduct additional research. Once, you find a reliable source, you must cite it. If you can't determine whether it is well known, you should cite it; this is known as the just-in-case rule to avoiding plagiarism.

4. How should I do parenthetical citations if I do not know which pieces of information come from which original source?

   Investigate each source to determine the origin of the sourced information. If you cannot determine what information comes from each source, you cannot use the source. You must document and cite correctly and completely.

5. Word automatically provides the documentation for my sources in APA and MLA format. Why do I have to learn how to document and cite?

   Actually organizing and formatting the paper will help you develop better determining skills, differentiating skills, connecting skills, and writing skills.

Glossary

A

Academic dishonesty—an intentional act of deception in which writers (students, professors, professionals, and lay writers) claim credit for the work or effort of another person, use unauthorized material, or fabricate information in any academic or professional work.

Academic honesty—following academic standards by completing, composing, documenting, and citing all academic work and admission criteria without misrepresentation.

Academic topic—choosing, discussing, and writing topics that display academic, post-secondary education rigor.

Alterations—changes to an original.

Attribution—correctly recognizing the original source of information used in composition, ideas, concepts, thought, and creation.

B

Blog—an electronic diary or journal that the blogger (writer) can share with millions of readers.

Byline—acknowledgement of the writer by including his/her name to an article.

C

Citation—acknowledging a source within the text (also known as in-text citation). A citation immediately follows text that has been quoted, paraphrased, or summarized. A citation for each quote, paraphrase, and summary is important because it signals the reader that the information is source generated.

Connotation—subjective, personal definition of a word.

D

Denotation—a concrete definition of the word. Denotation is often referred to as dictionary meaning.

Documentation—the bibliographic page, known as Works Cited for MLA (Modern Language Association) format or References for APA (American Psychology Association) format. Documentation includes the source information in its entirety (publisher, author, editor, web name, etc.).

F

Fair use—the percentage of sources that are allowable for a document.

H

Hashtag—also refer to as a pound sign (#) is used to categorize topics.

Hyperbolic—overly descriptive language.

I

Information literacy—understand where to search and the criteria to use to determine the best sources to use for objective, correct, and concise information.

Infringement—a company or individual using the exact or similar name, symbol, or mantra, so much so that it would cause confusion amongst consumers.

L

Lead-in phrase—an introduction to source information.

Lead-out phrase—a concluded statement following source information.

Literacy—the ability to understand and use language correctly and concisely.

M

Manipulation—to influence for one's own advantage or benefit.

O

Objective meaning—neutral and factual meaning; free from opinion.

P

Perfunctory—uninteresting or unfocussed information.

Plagiarism—literary theft; to steal words.

Pop culture—people, places, and things that are define as entertaining, known to be influential to a large segment of a nation's population.

R

Reliability—measures the credibility of a source.

Research fallacies—errors in logic that researchers use to interpret findings.

S

Sampling—applied to music, taking the original—the sample—and mixing it with different lyrics or music.

Scholarly articles—articles that appear in peer-reviewed journals.

Subjective meaning—one's personal interpretation.

Synthesize—combining ideas and facts to form a new single idea.

T

Tag—an attachment or marking on an object so that it can be identified as new or different.

V

Validity (internal and external validity)—the trustworthiness and truthfulness of research results.